YOU'RE *never too old* FOR ANYTHING

ABOUT THE AUTHOR

Anita Lutsenko is Ukraine's leading motivational speaker and go-to expert on maintaining a healthy lifestyle. Aged 16, she was awarded the title of Master of Sports in Sports Aerobics and won a silver medal at the European Championship. On top of this, she became a multiple-time champion of aerobics and fitness in her native Ukraine. Since then, she has moved on to perform as a presenter at Nike fitness conventions and has been a personal trainer for numerous celebrities, actors, and politicians.

In 2011, Anita became a trainer for participants hoping to lose weight on the show The Biggest Loser, broadcast on the Ukrainian channel STB. The audience fell in love with Anita for her professional approach and her remarkable charisma, leading to her landing the role of presenter for the show's seventh and ninth seasons.

In 2018, she was a contestant on the Ukrainian version of the world-famous television show Strictly Come Dancing. Later that same year, Anita became an ambassador for the Puma sportswear brand.

She has co-authored two books in collaboration with a nutritionist and a chef: You're Just Wow! and Let's do it quickly!

Additionally, she has appeared on the cover of Cosmopolitan and collaborated with Philips, Vichy, Coca-Cola, Bosch, and Samsung. Her YouTube channel offering expert advice on healthy living has more than one million subscribers and is one of the most popular fitness channels in Ukraine. Her Instagram account @anitasporty currently has 1.1 million followers.

Editor: Natalia Pasichnyk
Design: Antonina Latayko
Photo: Katerina Astrella, Mariana Shafro, Barney Hindle
Proofreading: Barney Ellis

You're never too old for anything / Anita Lutsenko. Kyiv 2024. – 144 pages.

Anita Lutsenko, a well-known fitness trainer and promoter of healthy living, gained her inspiration to create this book from the relationship she formed with Heather, her 75-year-old friend from Great Britain. Within each chapter of this book, you will discover a recipe for a delicious dish, a unique story from Heather's eventful life, as well as some interesting facts about the traditions, culture, and lifestyle of the British people. This book shows us that not only does life exist after 70, but that it can also be active, beautiful, and full of love and adventure!

All rights reserved. Any reproduction of the material, in whole or in part, is permitted only with the author's written permission.

This is an inspirational book. I like to call it a 'coffee table book'. It's about what inspires us, as women, to live, to be brave, to be happy, to get active and, most importantly, to not be ashamed of being happy at any age. At the age of 75, my great friend Heather completely embodies this spirit and it's thanks to her that this book exists. Each chapter consists of two parts: a recipe for a delicious dish from Heather and a story from her eventful life. And since Heather is from Great Britain, I have supplemented the book with some interesting and lesser – known facts about the traditions, culture, and daily life of the British, which we as Ukrainians can hopefully learn from. For me, this experience will stay with me forever. I now know it is possible to live a really good life into old age; it will be the example which I shall follow.

Anita

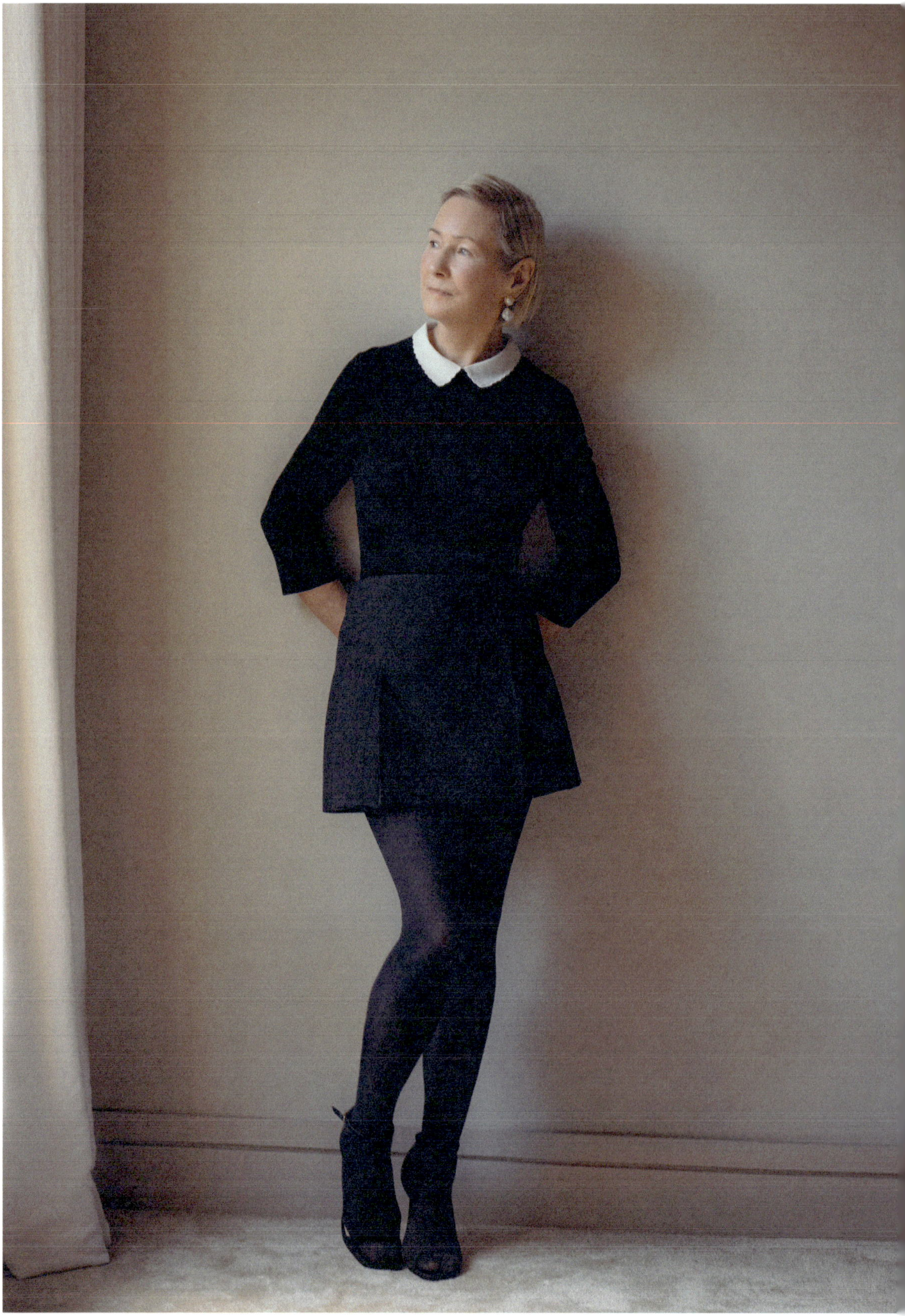

Never think that you are too old for something.
Heather Leikin, 75

content

27
Mint Jelly

DINNERS

30
Dinner 1. Fish Pie
Grandmother's Treats

38
Dinner 2. Curried Pear & Parsnip Soup
Why She Doesn't Eat Meat

49
Dinner 3. Filo Quiche with Feta and Leek
Family Traditions

52
Dinner 4. Turkey Quinoa Loaf
Work and Passions

60
Dinner 5. Fajitas
Living in America

66
Dinner 6. Lemon Chicken Pasta
Cooking as a Chore and Inspiration

74
Dinner 7. Super Taco Salad
Coffee for Breakfast and Her Health

80
Dinner 8. Pasta Puttanesca
Travelling to the Ends of the World

86
Dinner 9. Prawn Curry
Extreme Hobbies

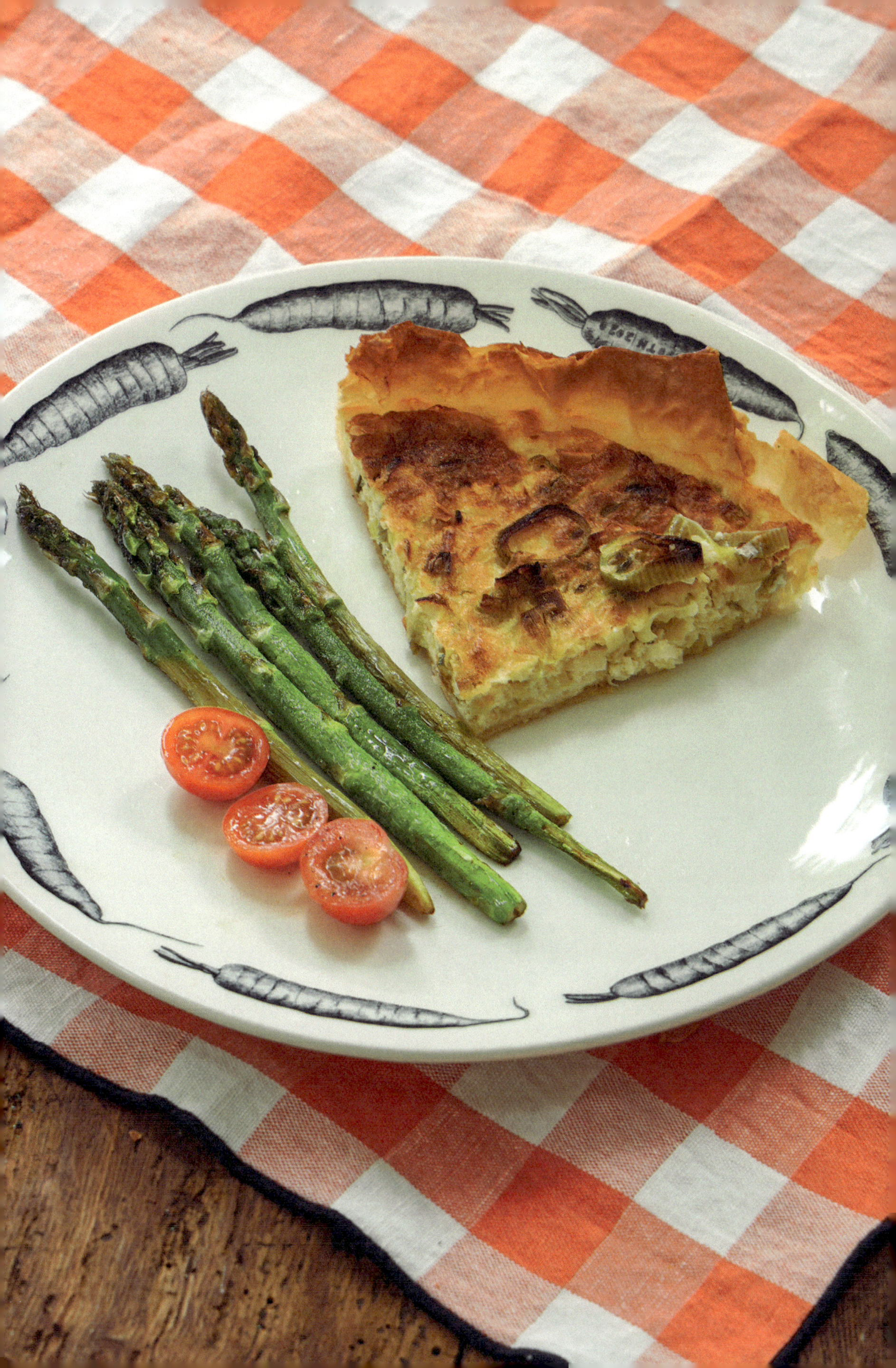

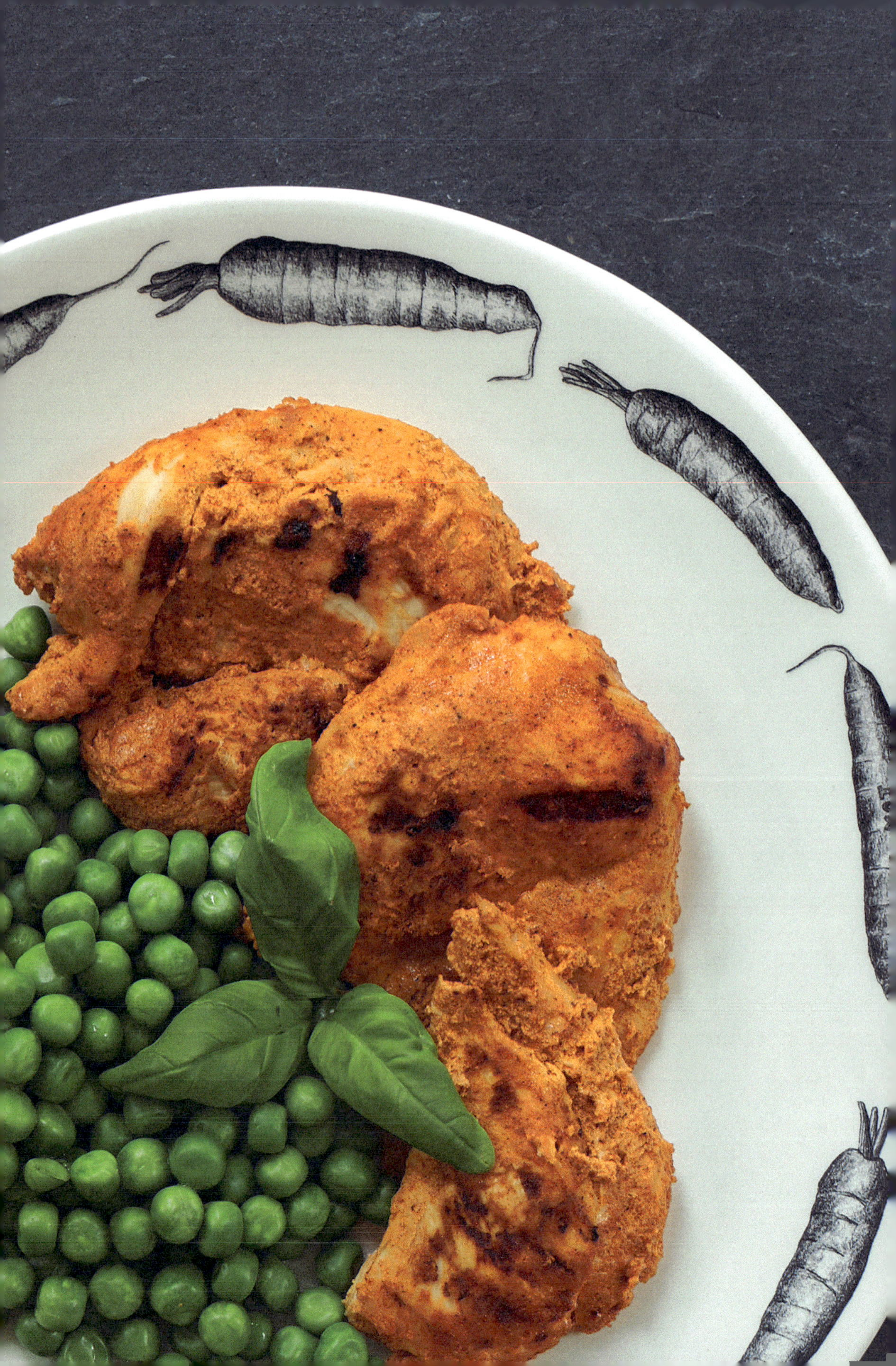

92
Dinner 10. Smoked Haddock Kedgeree
High Heels and Beauty Routine

98
Dinner 11. Thai Fish Cakes
Men, Dating and Relationships

104
Dinner 12. Celebration Chicken
Independence and Happiness

112
Dinner 13. Italian Sausage Bread
Children and Food

118
Dinner 14. Vegetarian Moussaka
Dancing and Friendship

124
Dinner 15. Tandoori Chicken
Weight and Carbohydrates Plus Top 5 Lunches

DESSERTS
130
Cranachan
Colourful Food and the UK's Cuisine

132
Eton Mess
Wine and the Tradition of Afternoon Tea

134
HRT Cake
The People of Great Britain

136
Lemon Cheesecake
Making the World a Better Place

140
Summer Pudding

I met Heather at the beginning of the war. Like thousands of other residents of Great Britain, she invited Ukrainians, about whom she knew nothing, into her home. That's how my 5-year-old daughter Mia and I ended up in a tiny, picturesque village south of London in the perfectly maintained house of a 75-year-old lady.

In those first weeks in England, I was somewhat saved from stress by time spent in the kitchen. I cooked a lot back then – syrnyky, pancakes, borscht, baked cakes. Heather tasted everything, and in return treated me to a few of her favourite meals, as well as some classic British dishes. We shared recipes and stories. Every day I became more and more interested in our host, who was not in the least bit like our traditional understanding of an 'elderly woman'.

Always elegant and slim, with a neat hairstyle and high heels, Heather was never tired and was always in perfect health. In all the time I stayed with her, I never once saw her take medicine, and never heard a single complaint about her well-being!

Besides this, Heather was always on the move. A two-hour walk every day, taking care of a large garden and house, meeting with friends, doing charity work. Often, a bright sports car would drive up to the porch, her latest boyfriend ready to whisk her off on a date to some fashionable restaurant.

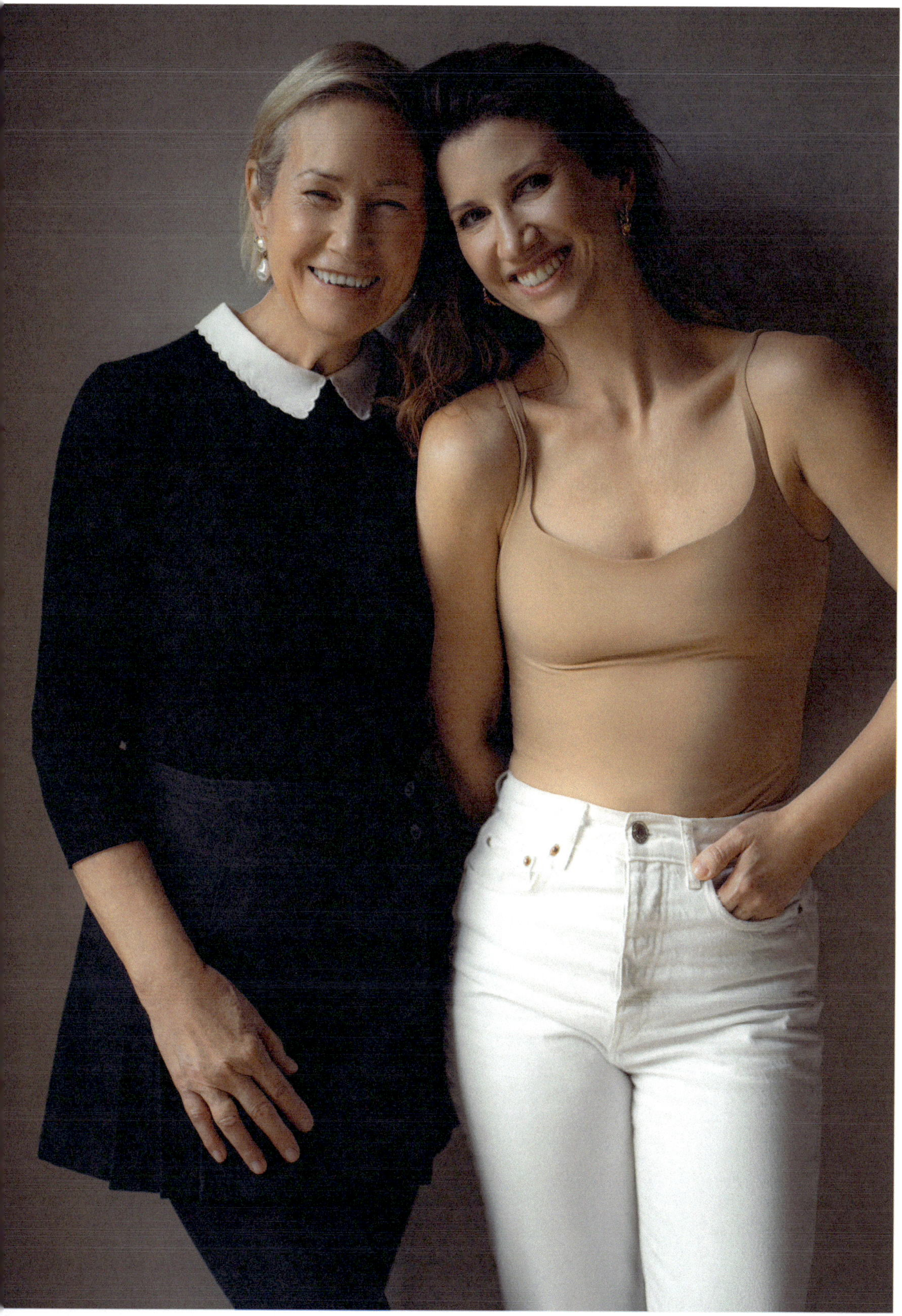

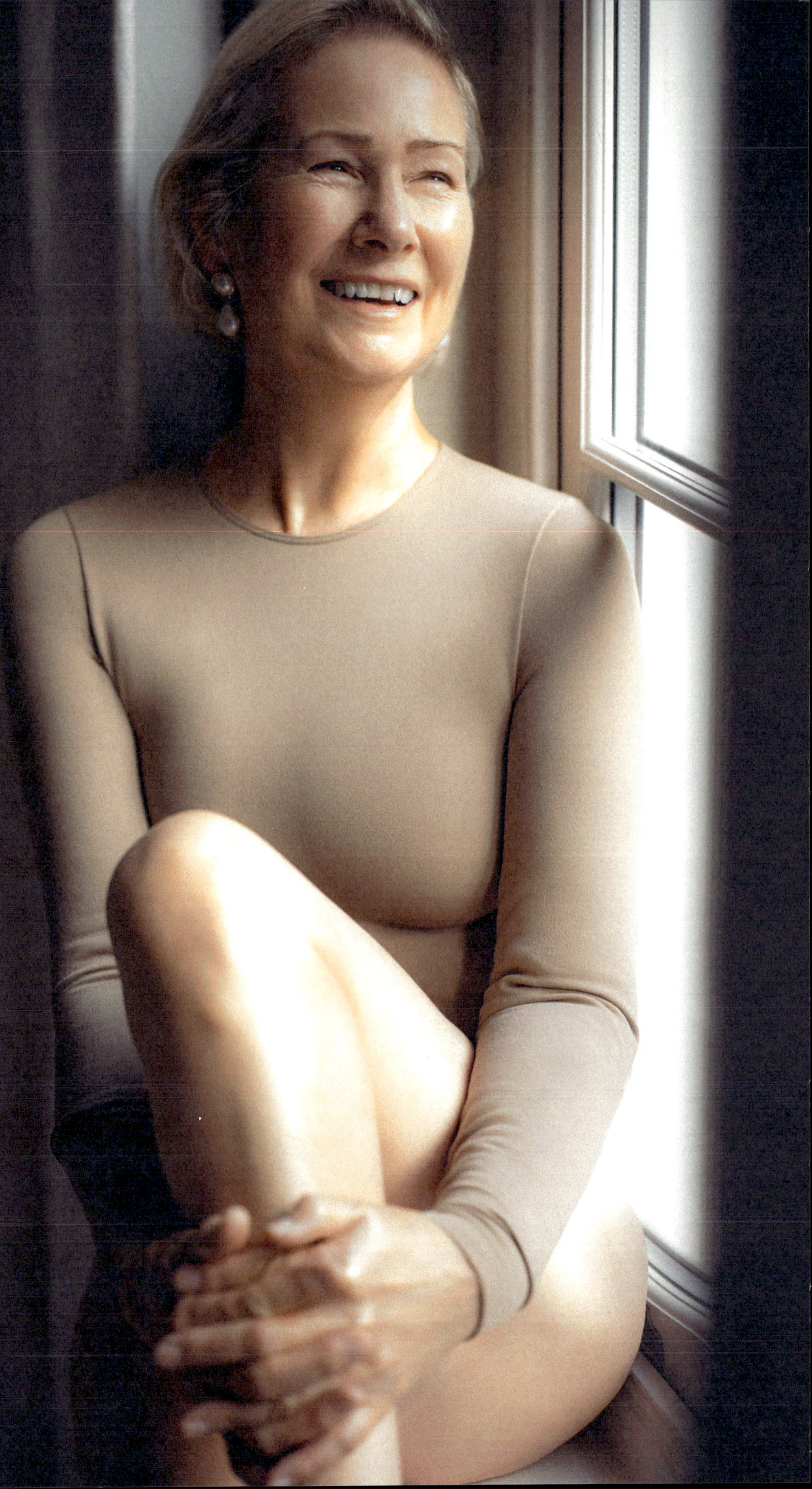

> **HEATHER NEVER *puts anything off* 'FOR LATER': THE WASHING MACHINE IS TURNED OFF — AND SHE IS *already hanging the clothes,* THE IRONING IS DONE AS SOON AS THEY ARE DRY. DISHES ARE WASHED AS SOON AS THE MEAL IS FINISHED. *There are no delayed actions.***

Despite growing up in the tough post-war years, Heather lives life as she pleases. She still remembers poverty, food and heating shortages, having to scrimp and save for everything. Perhaps this made her a person with strong discipline, who believes that there is no reason to miss school or work as long as you wake up in the morning. She worked in a bank almost all her life and didn't retire until she was in her 70s. However, this attitude towards life is characteristic of many of the British.

Another feature of the British mentality is that Heather knows what she will do tomorrow, in a month, in a year. Her calendar is planned far in advance. At the age of 75, she actively explores the world and tests her capabilities: she has walked on the wing of an aeroplane hundreds of metres above the ground, surfed in the ocean, launched herself off a mountain with a parachute. Having travelled almost the entire globe, she shows no signs of letting up. As I write this, she is planning her next trip to New Zealand.

Heather became for me a perfect example of the phrase, 'I can do it myself'. If something breaks in her house, a shelf needs putting up, or a pipe needs unblocking, she doesn't call a handyman, or any man. Heather thinks she's strong and smart enough to do it on her own. In her company

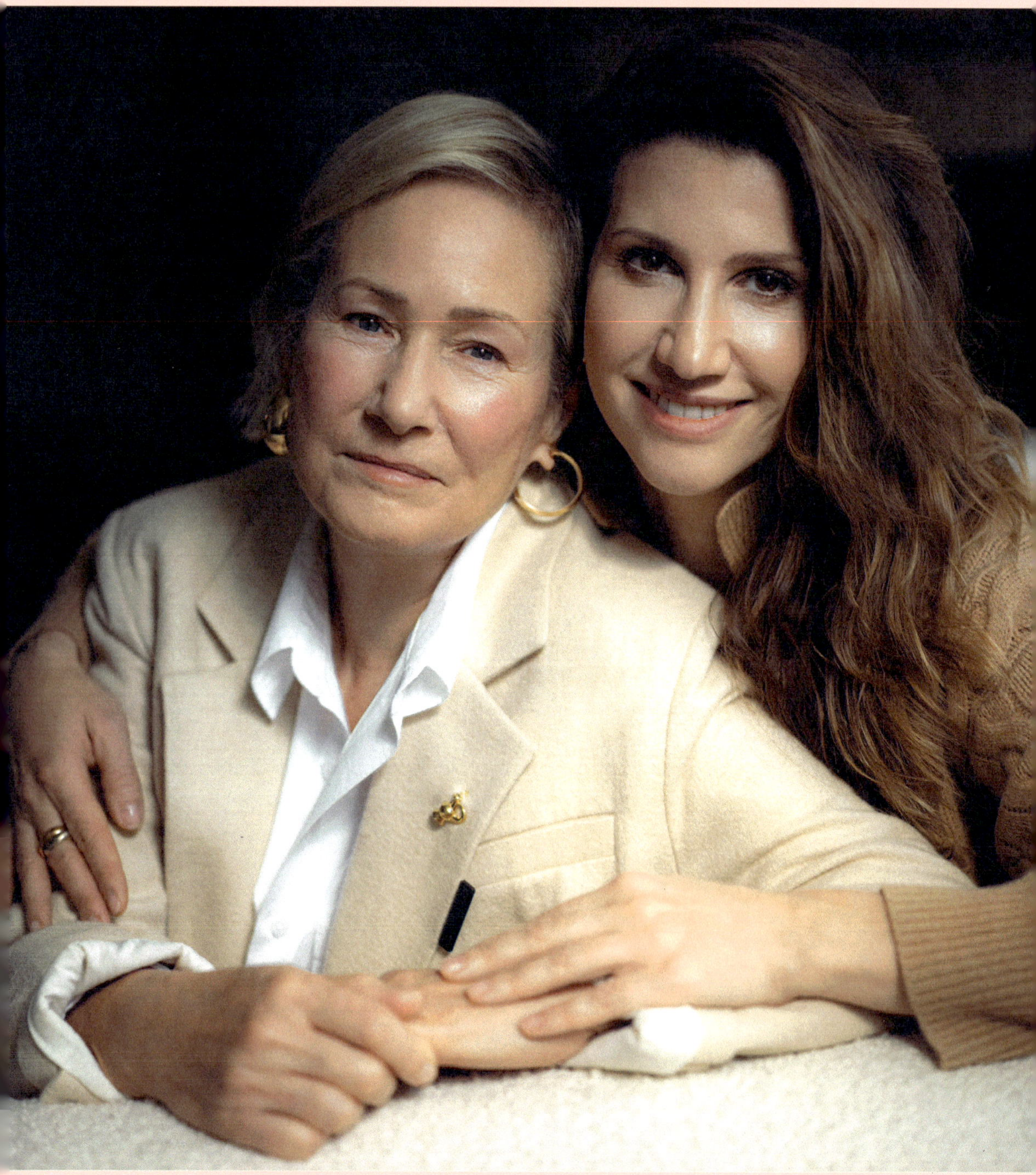

I felt very protected, but at the same time very aware of my own weaknesses. She doesn't see limits and doesn't want to depend on anyone. She can date men, but she is not going to marry a third time. She doesn't want to dissolve into the role of a grandmother, although this doesn't prevent her from adoring her grandchildren.

She likes to live for herself and surround herself with beauty. Every day she cooks something fancy for dinner. Heather's meals always look like art – bright, colourful, on warmed plates and impeccably served. At the same time, they are easy to cook, because in her opinion, the kitchen should be for fun, for pleasure.

Heather always knows what it takes to turn a meal from ordinary into something you want to dive straight into. Sometimes I took bread and cheese and asked her what to add. Immediately the refrigerator would open, a jar of caramelised onions or mango chutney, or some other spicy or sweet condiment would appear, and the sandwich would go from ordinary to incredible.

Heather feels young. That's what she is! Certainly, her good health, good looks, and bubbling energy have something to do with her diet. But this is not some boring diet. I would describe her daily menu as, 'a cup of coffee in the morning, a glass of wine in the evening, and in between – something colourful and freshly cooked'. Her recipes seem to speak of self-love, lightness and pleasure without becoming a 'cheat meal'.

By the way, the principles that Heather intuitively follows when it comes to food are consistent with what scientists say about how to stay young and live longer: don't overeat, eat plenty of vegetables, cut down on meat, etc. But let her tell you more about that herself in this book.

I think I caught myself thinking so often that I wanted to be like Heather 'when I grow up', that I finally got her to share some of her secrets about family traditions, extreme hobbies, men, raising children, happiness, work, passion, the cuisine of Great Britain and the lifestyle of modern Britons.

Every evening in Heather's kitchen was like a cooking reality show. I felt like I was living with Madonna or Oprah and I was able to learn – in depth and in detail. It's like getting access to a workshop from an icon, where you see everything as it really is – not staged, but unfiltered and with honesty.

Often, while waiting for the oven to beep 'ready', Heather would jump up to sit on the high kitchen workbench – sitting sexually cross-legged in a short skirt, with perfect knees, a glass of wine in one hand, talking and asking questions. And I was not ashamed to compliment her movements, her skin tone, every inch the figure and posture of a 30-year-old woman who knows her worth.

"
HEATHER *feels young.* THAT'S WHAT SHE IS!
I WOULD DESCRIBE HER DAILY MENU AS
'*a coffee in the morning,* A GLASS OF WINE
IN THE EVENING, AND IN BETWEEN — *something
colourful* AND FRESHLY COOKED.'

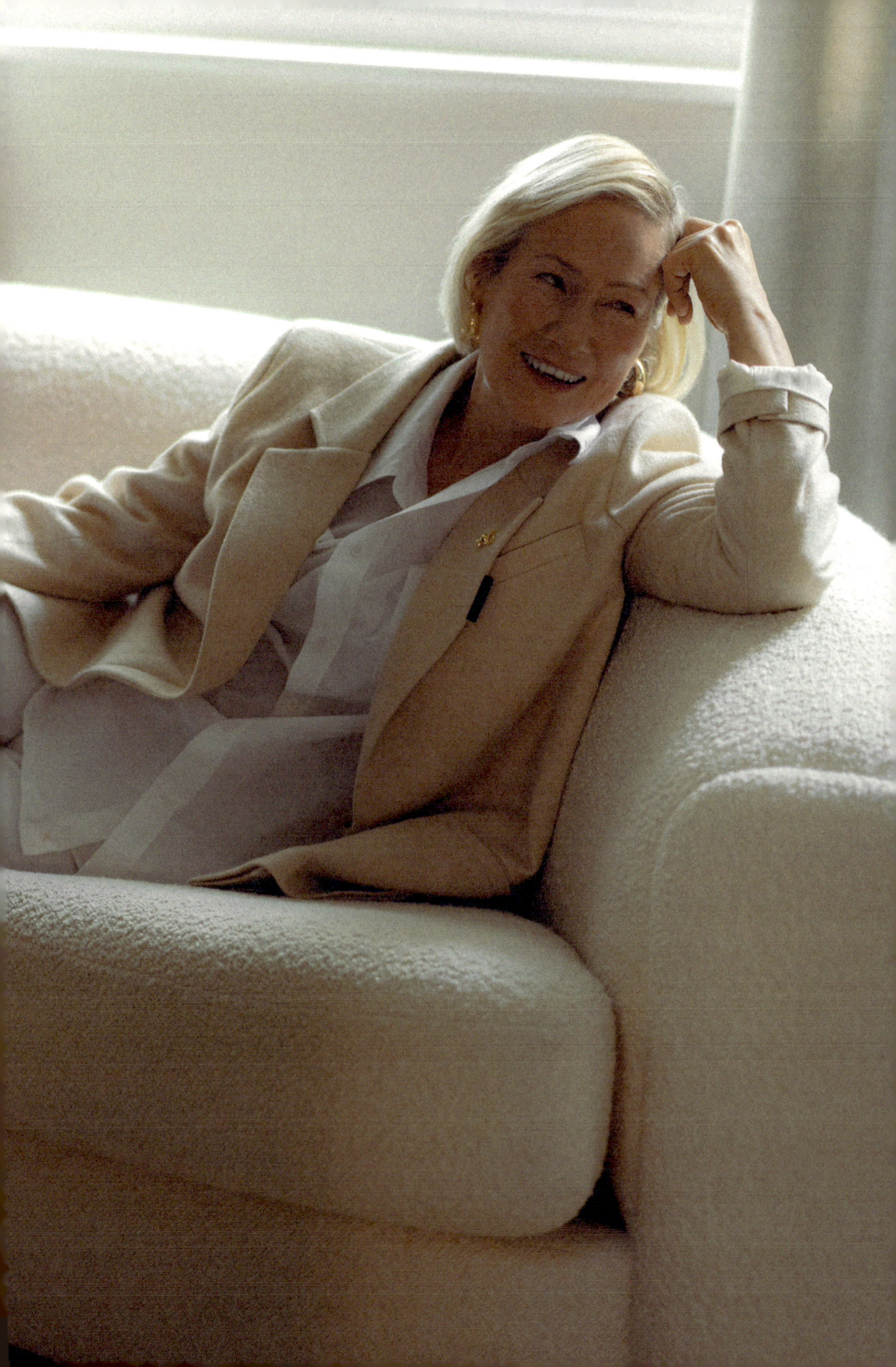

"

THE ABILITY TO *not complain about fatigue,* TO NOT GET COLD (SHORTS IN NOVEMBER ARE EASY) AND *not to run* TO THE PHARMACY WITH EVERY SNEEZE.

This is how our book about 15 dinners consisting of colourful meals and tasty desserts from a modern English lady appeared. Our 15 conversations on topics that would help me understand how I could be like her when I reach the age of 75. I soaked up everything like a sponge and really wanted to share it with my friends and followers.

I have to say that, in the beginning, many things in the United Kingdom seemed unusual to me. The impeccable politeness of the British, who really do apologise when someone steps on their toes! Obligatory small talk asking, 'How are you?' and always discussing the weather. Tea with milk. Fish poached in milk. Greeting cards for every occasion. Irresistible love of lotteries. The ability to refuse without actually saying the word 'no'.

But the more I learned, the more I wanted to take some of these peculiarities for my own life. For example, the ability to say, 'Thank you'. To start sending those thank you cards that children and adults write to each guest after their birthday with warm words about their gift. The ability to queue. The skill of planning in advance. The ability not to complain about fatigue, not to get cold *(shorts in November are easy)* and not to run to the pharmacy with every sneeze. The culture of sharing with others and helping those in need as an integral part of life.

So, welcome to Heather's kitchen! I hope that in addition to the new cool recipes, you, like me, will be imbued with her zest for life and desire to make this world a little better.

Anita

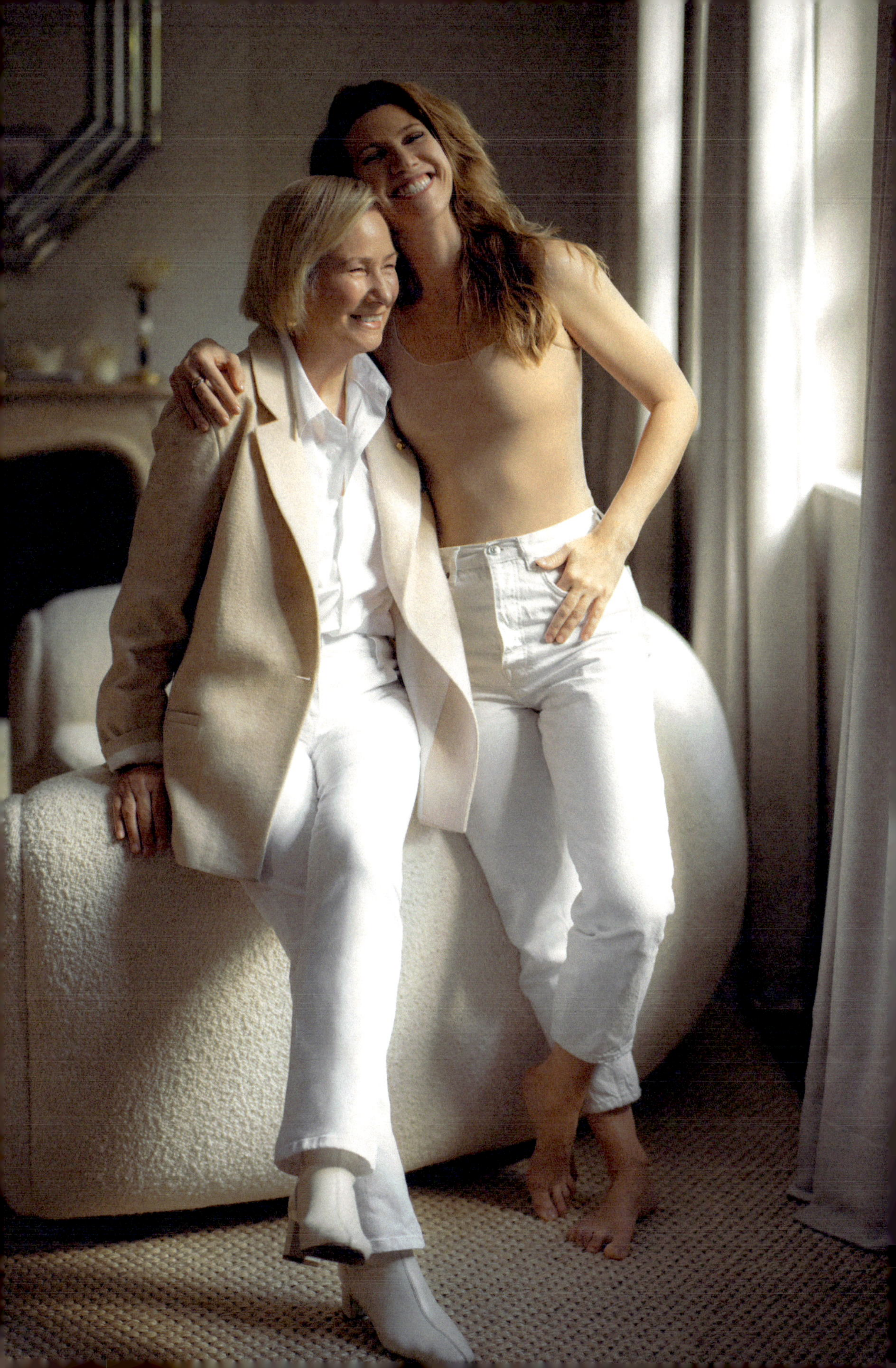

" HEATHER HAS *never had any cosmetic treatments,* YET HER SKIN LOOKS LIKE SHE'S 40. SHE JOKES THAT *she's like a mummy,* PRESERVED FROM THE INSIDE BY ALCOHOL.

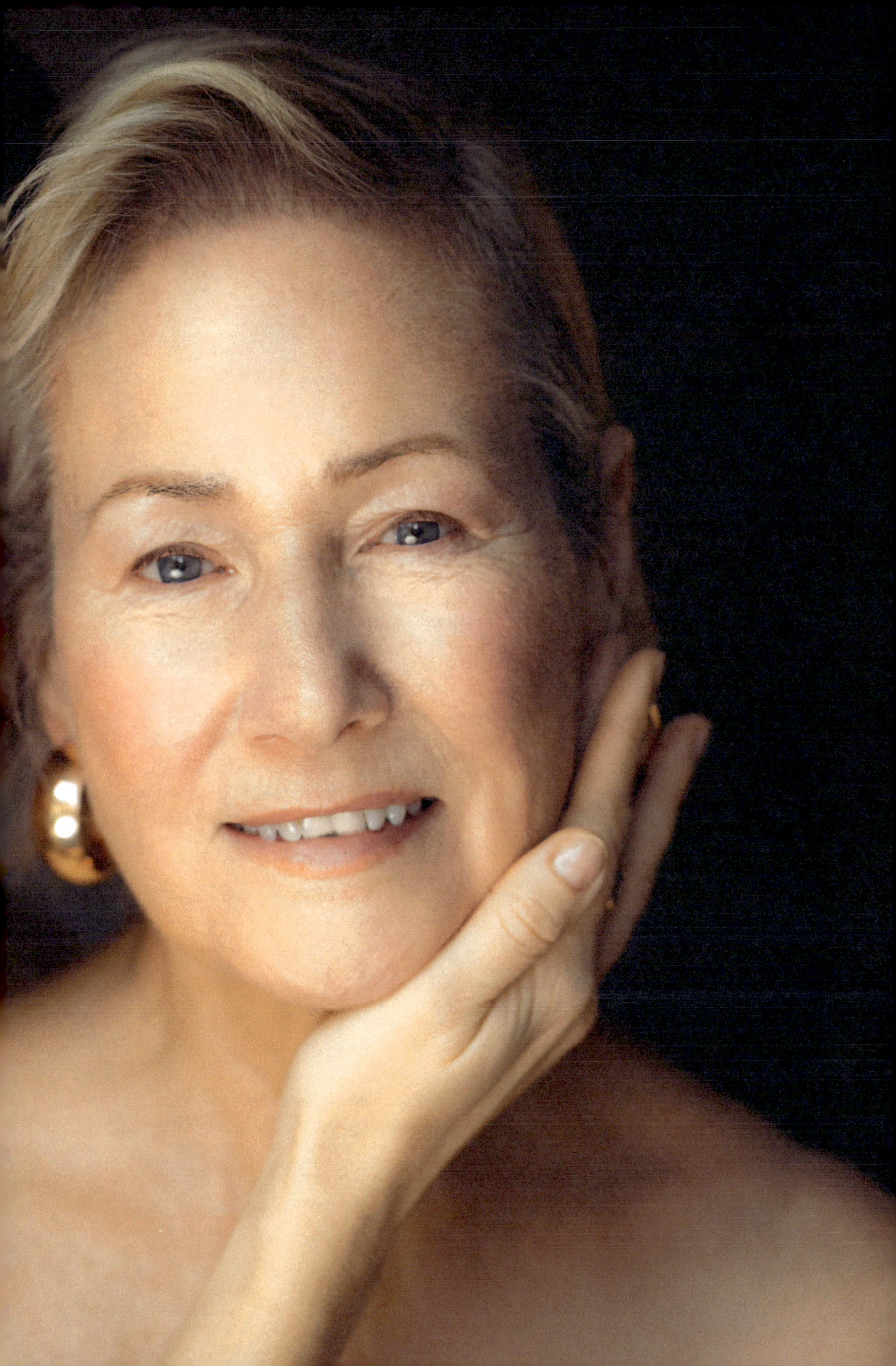

TO START WITH...

Here is one thing that surprised me and inspired me to start collecting recipes and stories from Heather. That thing is mint jelly.

When Heather first served the green jelly with baby potatoes, I wrinkled my nose with a smile: a jelly? After all, baby potatoes should be eaten with butter and dill, after shaking them in a pot with a closed lid. But I was wrong. And soon I couldn't imagine potatoes without mint jelly, because it's a genius combination. One I love. The British usually buy it ready-made in a jar, like mustard or ketchup, but you can also prepare it yourself.

By the way, I think that sometimes we show too actively when we don't like something. In Great Britain, I understood, even if you don't like or want something, you can always say thank you with a smile and not eat it. This is upbringing. It is not necessary to visibly express your negative emotions.

What do the British do when they don't want something? Instead of a categorical 'No', they will say, 'I'm fine, thank you'. This is how even four-year-old children answer the question of whether they want food or water. And this is a completely different approach! Although, to be honest, I only manage to answer in the British style about two out of ten times, but I practise. I love how easy and casual it sounds.

Ukrainians are proud of our straightforwardness, but aren't we creating too much negativity around us this way? Smile, say thank you, take something else. No need to deceive anyone, just be simpler and more positive – it's cool.

This is an accompaniment almost solely used with lamb or new potatoes. It is easily purchased ready – made in the U.K., but here is an easy recipe to make it at home.
The green food colouring is traditional but not essential, as it tastes the same with or without it. It will be a soft golden colour if not used.

Mint Jelly

SERVES 4

2 large handful fresh mint fresh mint leaves packed down
600 ml boiling water
2 tbsp lemon juice
2 drops green food colouring
200 g white sugar
90 ml liquid pectin

1. Rinse the mint leaves and put them into a medium saucepan. Mash them with a potato masher and add the boiling water. Cover and let stand for 10 minutes.
2. Strain the mint mixture, reserving the liquid. Put 400 ml of this infusion back into the saucepan with the lemon juice, food colouring, and sugar.
3. Bring to a boil, stirring constantly. Stir in the pectin and boil for 1 minute, again stirring constantly.
4. Remove from the heat and skim off the foam from the top using a large metal spoon. Transfer the mint mixture to sterile jars and seal.
5. Place the jars on a rack inside a large pan of boiling water, making sure the water level is at least one inch above the tops of the jars. Bring the water to a full boil, cover the pot, and leave to boil for 10 minutes.

When I tried this dish, I felt both delight and... indignation. How did it happen that we, big connoisseurs of mashed potatoes, do not know this recipe?! It is brilliant! Tasty, simple and elegant. This pie is always in Heather's freezer in case she needs to whip up a quick dinner. Put it in the oven – and it's ready.

DINNER 1

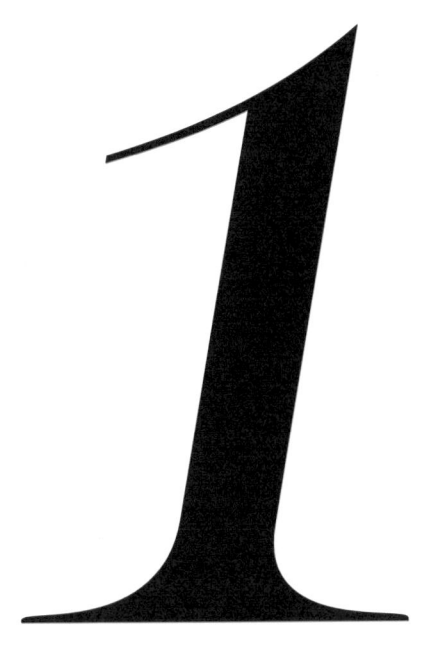

Fish Pie

It is a comforting and hearty supper for those cold winter nights and every family in England has their own version of this classic dish. Here is a basic recipe and at the bottom of the page, a list of substitutions/additions that you can use to make your own favourite version.

SERVES 4

1 kg potatoes
600 ml milk
400 g skinless boneless cod
400 g skinless boneless smoked haddock
200 g raw king prawns, peeled
100 g butter
100 g cheddar cheese, grated
50 g plain flour
1 bay leaf
1 tbsp parsley, chopped

1. First, peel and chop the potatoes into chunks and boil until soft, then mash with half the butter.
2. While the potatoes are cooking, poach the white fish and smoked haddock in the milk with the bay leaf for about 10 minutes, or until the fish is cooked and flakes easily.
3. Strain the milk from the fish through a sieve and put aside to cool. Arrange the flaked cooked fish and prawns in a baking dish.
4. Next, make a basic white sauce by melting the remaining butter in a saucepan, then add the plain flour and stir until mixed.
5. Remove the pan from the heat and gradually add the cold reserved milk a little at a time and mix well until you have smooth sauce. Return to the heat and bring to the boil until thickened, then add the chopped parsley and ½ the cheese.
6. Pour the sauce over the fish. Top the dish with mashed potato and finish by sprinkling the rest of the cheese on top and season with pepper.
7. Bake in an oven at 200°C (180°C fan) for 30 minutes.

Use any firm white fish or salmon or add roughly chopped hard boiled eggs, peas or sweetcorn to the fish layer. Similarly, use dill instead of parsley or skip the herbs altogether from the sauce.

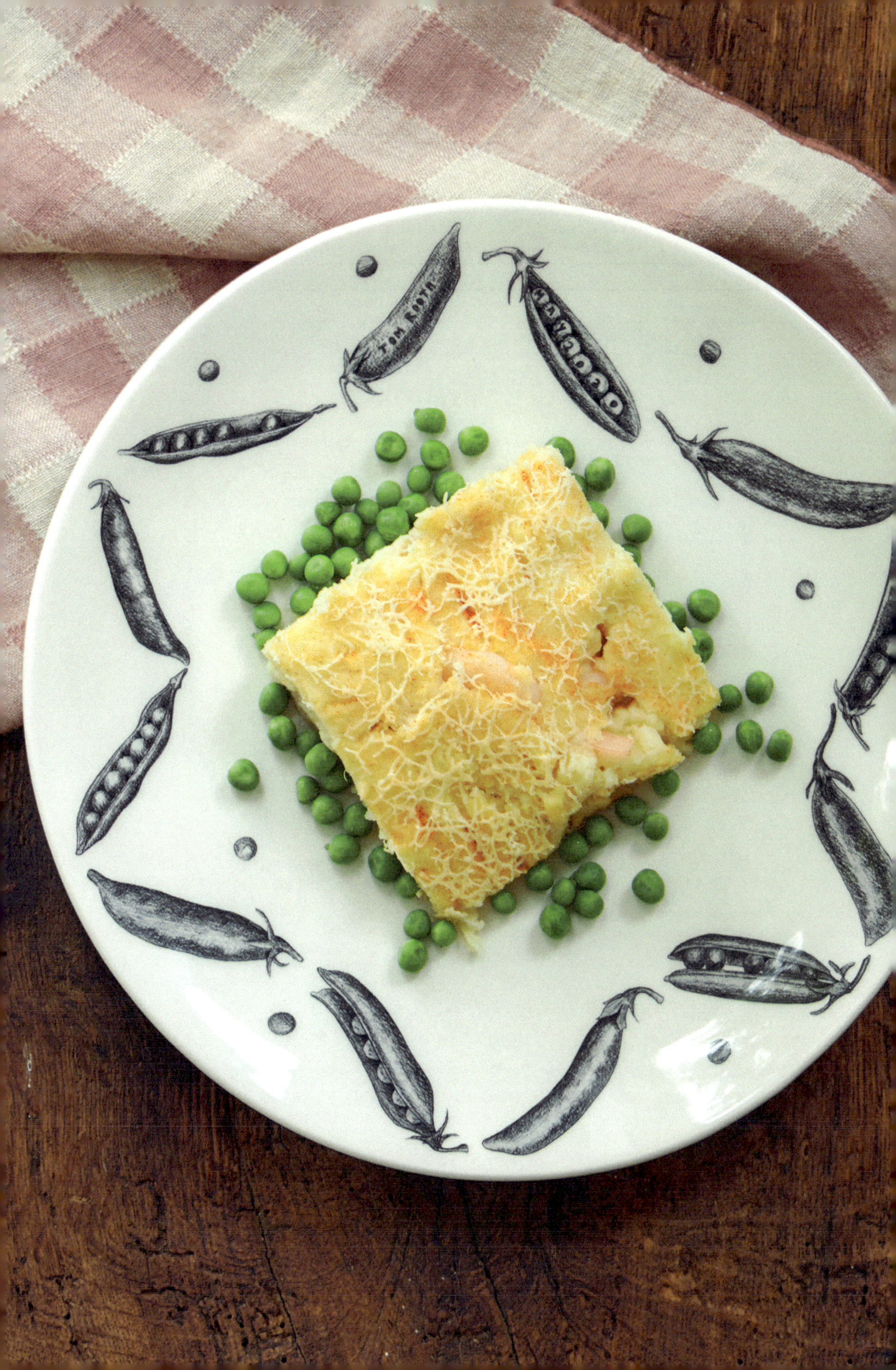

Grandma

Heather talks

GRANDMOTHER'S TREATS

I grew up in a small family. My grandad died when I was only three. My mother was always out at work, so it was my grandmother who brought me up. She was a very Victorian lady, very clever but quite disadvantaged. She had to leave school at twelve because her family was very poor. She played the piano, never being taught, but she could just sit down and play anything. Also, my grandmother was a brilliant cook, who could create meals out of nothing. And everything she made was perfect. I never saw her weigh or measure anything, she always did it with her eyes.

When I came home from school my grandma would have made a sponge cake. It would rise so high! She would slice the top off and I would get the hot cake as it came out of the oven. She would make me toffee apples and all sorts of treats. I remember the first thing that I thought when she died, 'I'll never taste one of her roast dinners again'. Sounds selfish, I know. I was 14. She tried to teach me to cook and I was always like, 'No, I'm going out to play'. When she passed away, I was devastated that I hadn't listened.

I do have a little book of recipes that she wrote but when I look at them, they are not really today's recipes. They use things that I wouldn't use now. Now my meals are much lighter and I don't eat meat. But the memory of my grandmother, her food and her love, will forever remain with me.

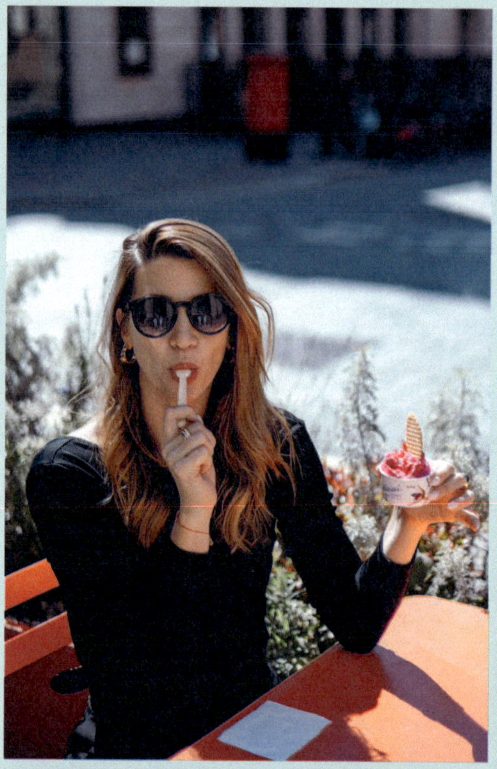
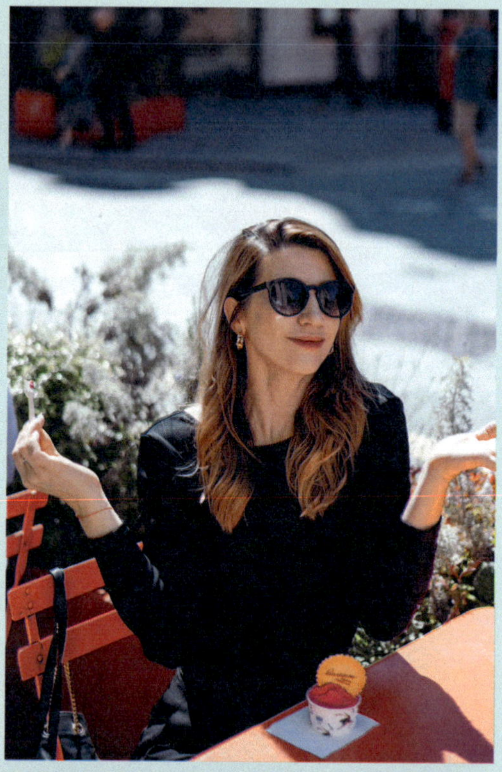
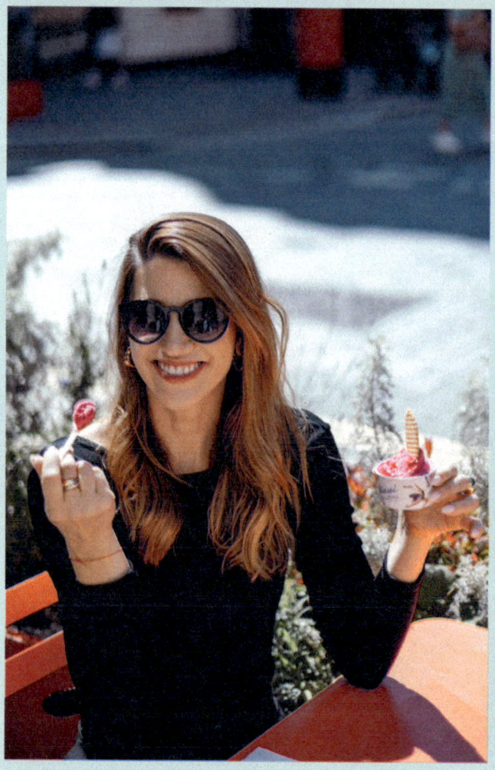
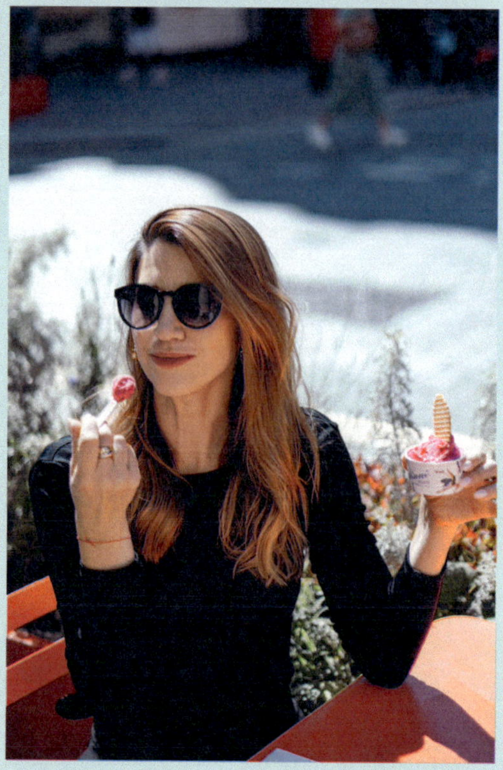

Did you know that...

Traditionally British cuisine has been perceived as heavy, bland and greasy, and something even mocked by the British themselves. Is it so awful? Yes, if it's not cooked properly. In supermarkets, the ready-meal sections are still the most popular. But in recent years, especially since the Covid-19 pandemic, locals have begun to pay more attention to food, to cook at home more often, and have made great progress with their cuisine. And some even cook like top chefs!

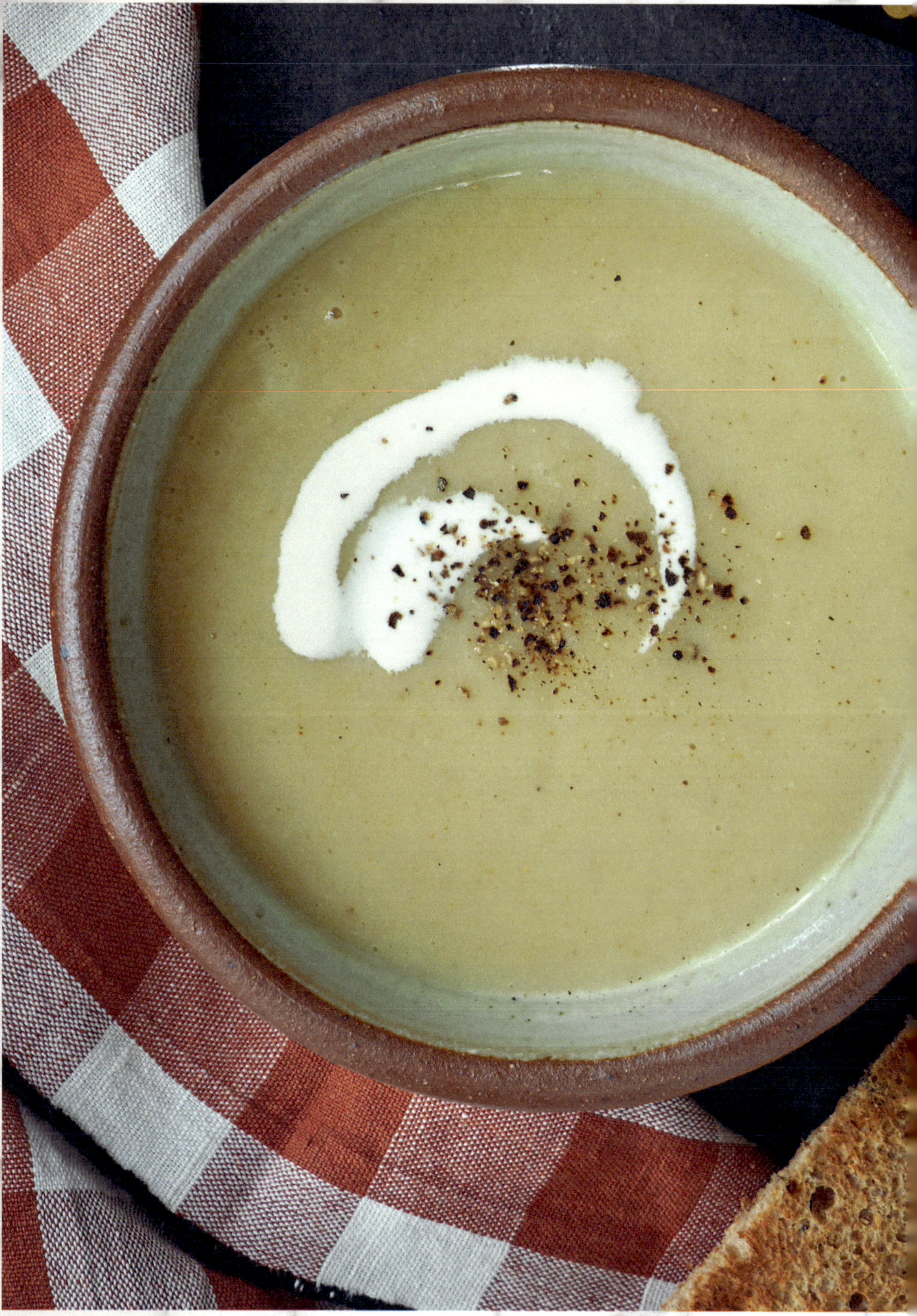

DINNER

2

Curried Pear & Parsnip Soup

We jokingly call it 'my' soup because I won't give it to anyone –
I eat it all myself! This hearty, spicy soup makes a wonderfully warming winter
meal when served with crusty bread. It has been such a favourite with
Heather's family that she always makes a double batch so that she can freeze
some in zip-lock bags for later use.

900 ml chicken stock
350 g parsnip, peeled and chopped
2 under-ripe pears, peeled, cored and chopped
1 onion, chopped
50 g butter
3 rashers of streaky bacon, chopped
1 celery stick, chopped
1 tbsp flour
1 tbsp curry powder
Salt & pepper

1. Melt the butter in a saucepan.
2. Add the onion and bacon and soften over a gentle heat.
3. Add the parsnips, pears and celery and cook for 10 minutes or so.
4. Stir in the flour and curry powder and then pour in the stock.
5. Cover and simmer for approximately 30 minutes until the parsnips are soft.
6. Blend until smooth and creamy.
7. Serve hot.

*When Heather makes this soup for herself, she doesn't use bacon.
And I like to sprinkle feta cheese on top.*

It has been such a favourite with Heather's family that she always makes a double batch so that she can freeze some in zip-lock bags for later use.

Heather and I have a very similar sense of humour. We joke all the time, although we often cry. Heather is a very empathetic person. Each of our long conversations or fleeting chats was always spiced up with friendly jokes, without insults or sideways glances. In general, for Heather, laughter, jokes and teasing are an integral part of the day. No fuss or discontent.

Everything is done with ease and kindness. I still can't believe how I can be so much on the same page with a person who is much older than me. I once read: in order for an older person to be treated with respect and to listen to their advice, they must be admired. With Heather, I felt this effect and wondered if, at 75, I would be enthralling my own grandchildren.

Red meat is a probable carcinogen. The International Fund for Research on Cancer *(IARC)* recommends consuming no more than 350–500 g of cooked red meat *(525–700 g raw)* per week, and that processed meat *(sausages, bacon, ham, etc.)* should be consumed minimally, or excluded from the menu altogether. Eat enough vegetables and have a few days each week without red meat *(this is all types of mammalian meat: beef, veal, pork, lamb, etc.).*

Heather talks

WHY SHE DOESN'T EAT MEAT

When I was little, I used to open the larder door and see the joint of meat for the roast on Sunday and it used to make me cry because I kept thinking about the poor animals that died. I didn't really like the taste and texture of meat in my mouth.

When I grew older, I married an American guy. He had a cholesterol problem, which we tried to control with his diet. Being American he liked BBQ steaks and ate lots of red meat. I managed to persuade him that we didn't need to do that, that we could eat much more healthily. We did it for a year and then we changed his diet forever. So that's when I started to use plant-based meat – to concentrate more on vegetarian food. It was great for me, I think. And I've been doing this since the 1990s.

I do eat chicken occasionally but not very often. I love fish. I've always liked cheese and vegetables. There is no vegetable I wouldn't eat.

Growing up as I did after the war, we had rationing for the first 5 years of my life so we had almost nothing except seasonal vegetables or things we could grow ourselves. No sweets, no exotic fruits. I remember there were no bananas in my early years. We just didn't get them after the war. We didn't have a refrigerator, so my grandmother would shop for food every day. Frozen food just didn't exist. It was a different childhood.

That evening, Heather suggested we watch a documentary called Coco, about a gorilla who was taught to use sign language from a young age. Are the feelings of animals and people different? No! Animals understand everything. Like people, they feel love, grief, fear, humour. Will I ever become a vegetarian? I think so.

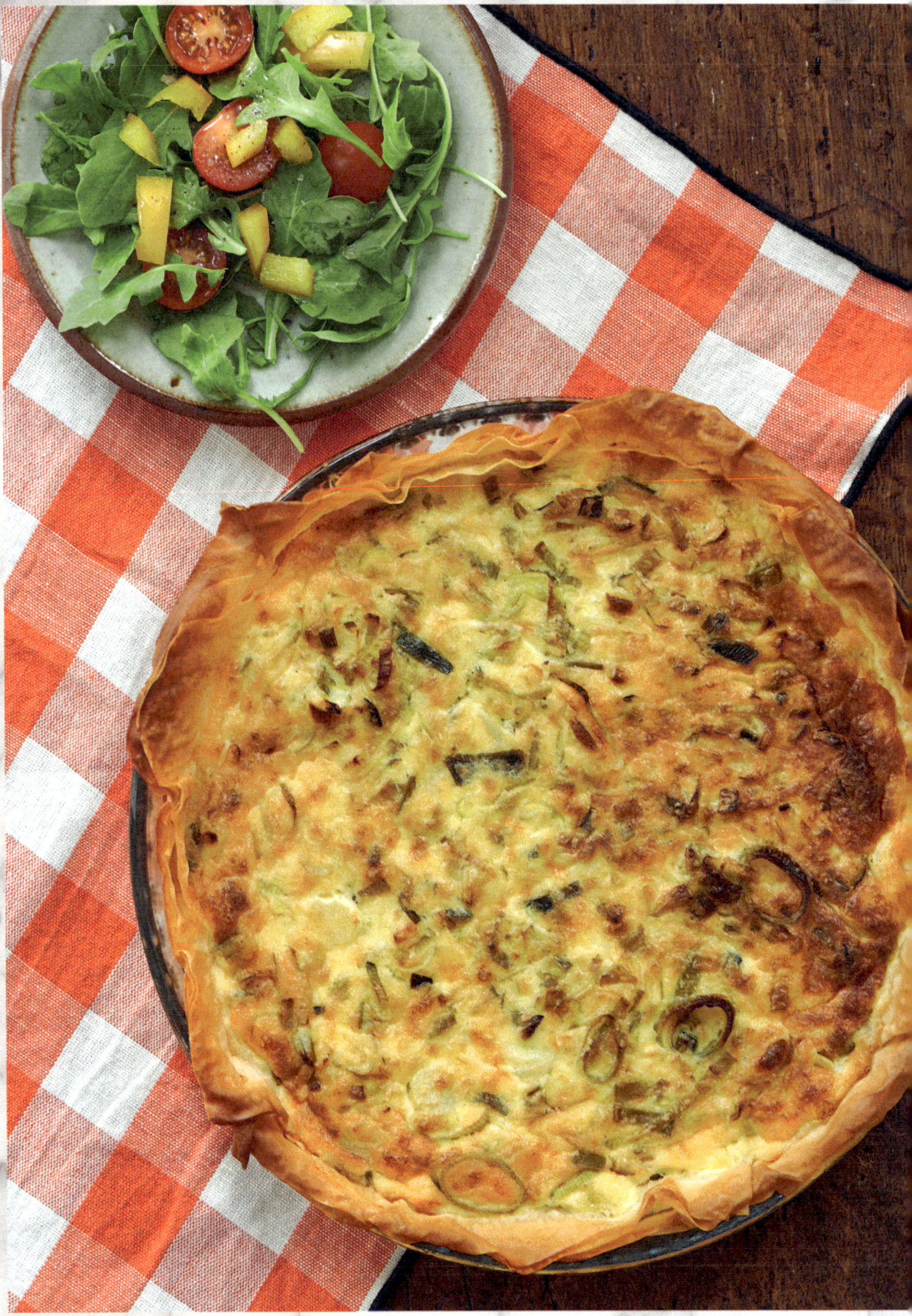

DINNER
3

Filo Quiche with Feta and Leek

This is one of Heather's favourite meals for lunch or dinner with friends. Using filo pastry for the base of this quiche makes it a lighter option than the traditional pastry version. It is relatively quick to make too.
And it smells really good when it's cooking!

SERVES 4

4 sheets of packaged filo pastry *(270 g package)*
4 small leeks / cooked broccoli *(well drained)*
150 ml cream
125 g feta cheese, finely grated
90 g butter
3 eggs, lightly beaten
1 clove of garlic
Salt & pepper

1. Melt 45 g of butter and use to brush each sheet of filo.
2. Then, fold each sheet in half and line an 18 cm quiche dish. Trim the edges leaving them standing approximately 1 cm above the edge of the dish.
3. Trim and wash the leeks and thinly slice. Melt the rest of butter in a pan, add the sliced leeks and crushed garlic and cook gently until soft. Add the grated cheese, cream and lightly beaten eggs. Mix well and season with pepper.
4. Pour the mix into the pastry case and bake about 170°C for approximately 30 minutes, or until golden brown.

If using cooked broccoli, just soften the garlic on its own before adding the well-drained broccoli with the cheese, cream and eggs.

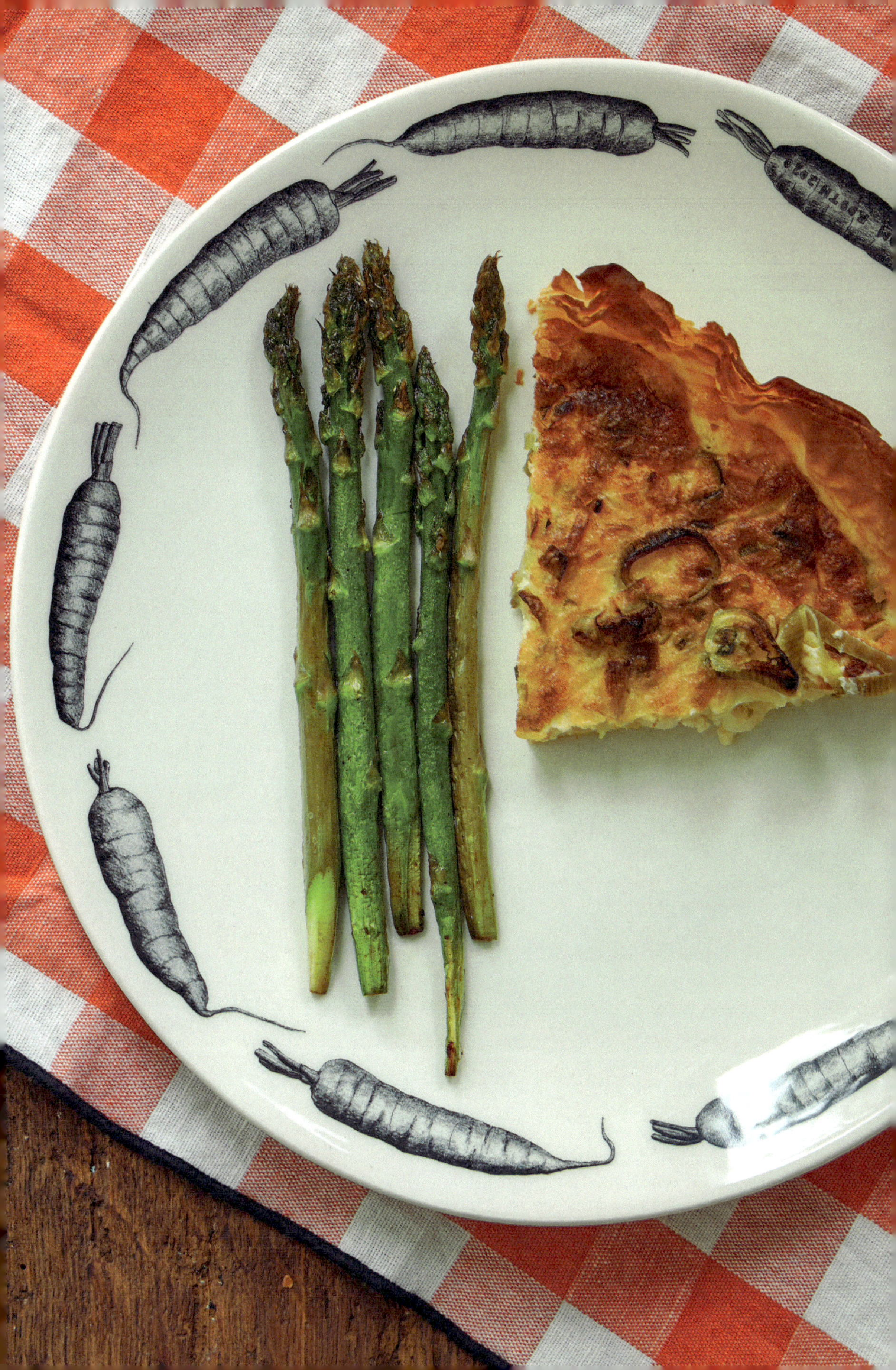

At Christmas in the family circle, I had to taste a dessert that was on fire because of the amount of alcohol inside! Everyone eats it, including children. To say that I was shocked is an understatement. I would call this dessert 'Sip of Whisky'

Heather talks

FAMILY TRADITIONS

My family now is my son, my daughter-in-law and two grandchildren. They live on the Isle of Wight. It's the largest island in England and has been a popular holiday destination since Victorian times. I see them quite often, about once every five to six weeks. They like coming here for a weekend, or I go over there. It's actually easier for me to go to the island than bringing them over here, as my son and his wife are both working. And it's better for me too, because cooking for them is a real disaster!

Why? Well, imagine, there are four of them and each of them wants something different. My daughter-in-law Deborah and 14-year-old granddaughter Alice do not eat fish or meat at all. 10-year-old Oscar eats everything and loves meat. My son used to be vegetarian but had to change his diet. So now he eats chicken and fish like me occasionally. Also, they are always on some crazy diets. I remember the sugar free diet, vegan diet – oh that was the worst, I lost the will to live there! Yes, children can make life difficult for me. When we have breakfast together, it's total chaos. For example, Oscar likes eggs and toast, cut into strips to dip in yolk. Alice eats cereal with oat milk. Daniel doesn't eat breakfast at all, and neither do I. And Deborah chooses something sweet in the morning – a cinnamon bun or a chocolate bar.

Although there is one dish that we all love – the Sunday roast. Traditionally, it consists of roast meat and roast potatoes with various vegetables, gravy and sauce. We replace meat with its plant-based alternatives. We always drink sherry while preparing the roast on Sunday morning, as well as at Christmas when we drink sherry by the fire while unwrapping our presents. We are very old fashioned about those traditions.

Sunday roast season finishes at Easter – we don't do it afterwards because nobody wants to be in the kitchen on a nice summer day. It's a winter thing. In the summer we like BBQs, that's another family tradition which we got from America.

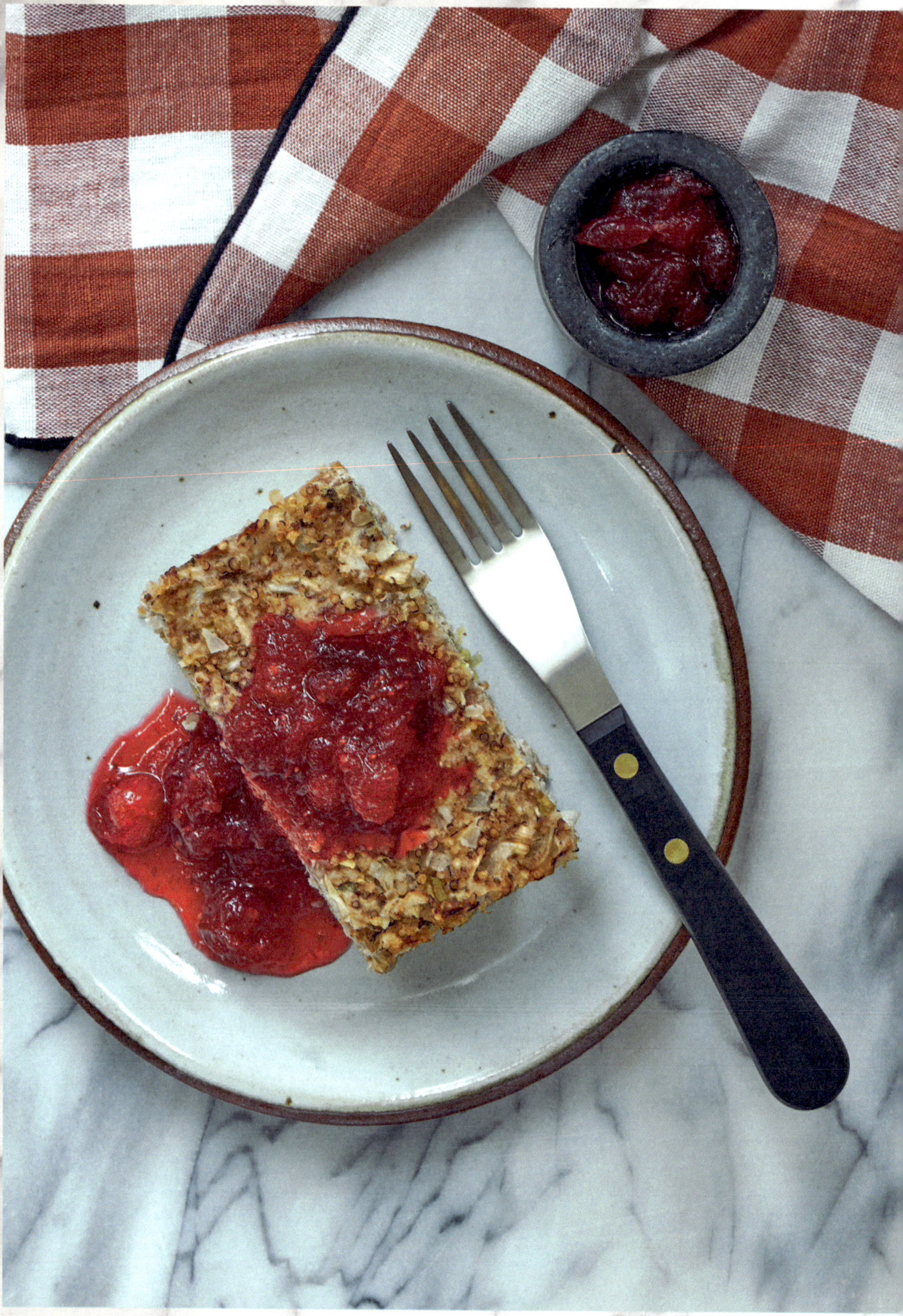

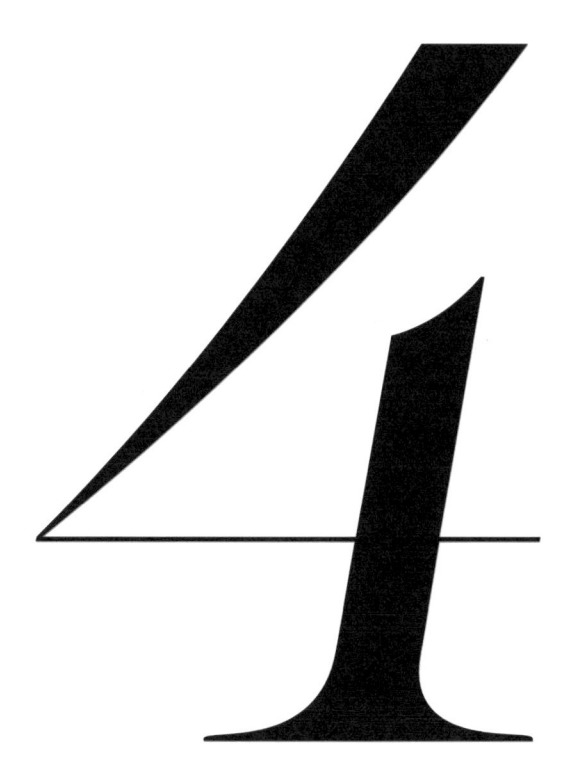

DINNER

4

Turkey Quinoa Loaf

Meatloaf combines everything you want to feed your family: protein, vegetables, grains, you name it. I like this version for the mix of nutty quinoa flavour and sweet and sour apple.

SERVES 6

250 g turkey mince
85 g quinoa, rinsed and drained
1 apple, peeled and grated
1 onion, finely chopped
1 egg, beaten
3 spring onions, chopped
2 tbsp fresh sage leaves, finely chopped
1 clove of garlic, finely chopped
1 tsp Worcestershire sauce
1 tsp sea salt
½ tsp freshly ground black pepper
¼ tsp ground allspice

CRANBERRY & ORANGE SAUCE

340 g fresh or frozen cranberries
150 g + 2 tbsp sugar
120 ml water
120 ml fresh orange juice
Zest of 1 orange

1. Toast the quinoa in a frying pan over a medium heat for 5 minutes or until fragrant and beginning to pop.
2. In a small saucepan bring 250 ml of salted water to the boil. Add the toasted quinoa, then cover and simmer over a medium heat for 15-20 minutes or until the water has been absorbed. Set aside.
3. Preheat the oven to 180°C and in a large bowl mix together the turkey, apple, onion, spring onion, garlic, sage, Worcestershire sauce, seasoning, spices and beaten egg. Add the quinoa and mix thoroughly.
4. Pack the mixture into a nonstick 1-litre loaf tin. Bake for 1 hour or until a meat thermometer registers 70°C when inserted in the centre of the meatloaf.
5. While the loaf is baking, you have time to make the sauce. In a medium saucepan boil water, orange juice and sugar.
6. When it boils add the cranberries, orange zest and salt, and return to the boil. Reduce the heat and simmer gently for 10-12 minutes until most of the cranberries have burst.
7. Transfer to a clean dish to cool. This will keep for 10 days covered in the fridge or 2 months in the freezer.
8. Serve the loaf with cranberry & orange sauce and your favourite salad.

This recipe was given to Heather by her close friend who sadly died from breast cancer. When Heather makes it, she always thinks of her.

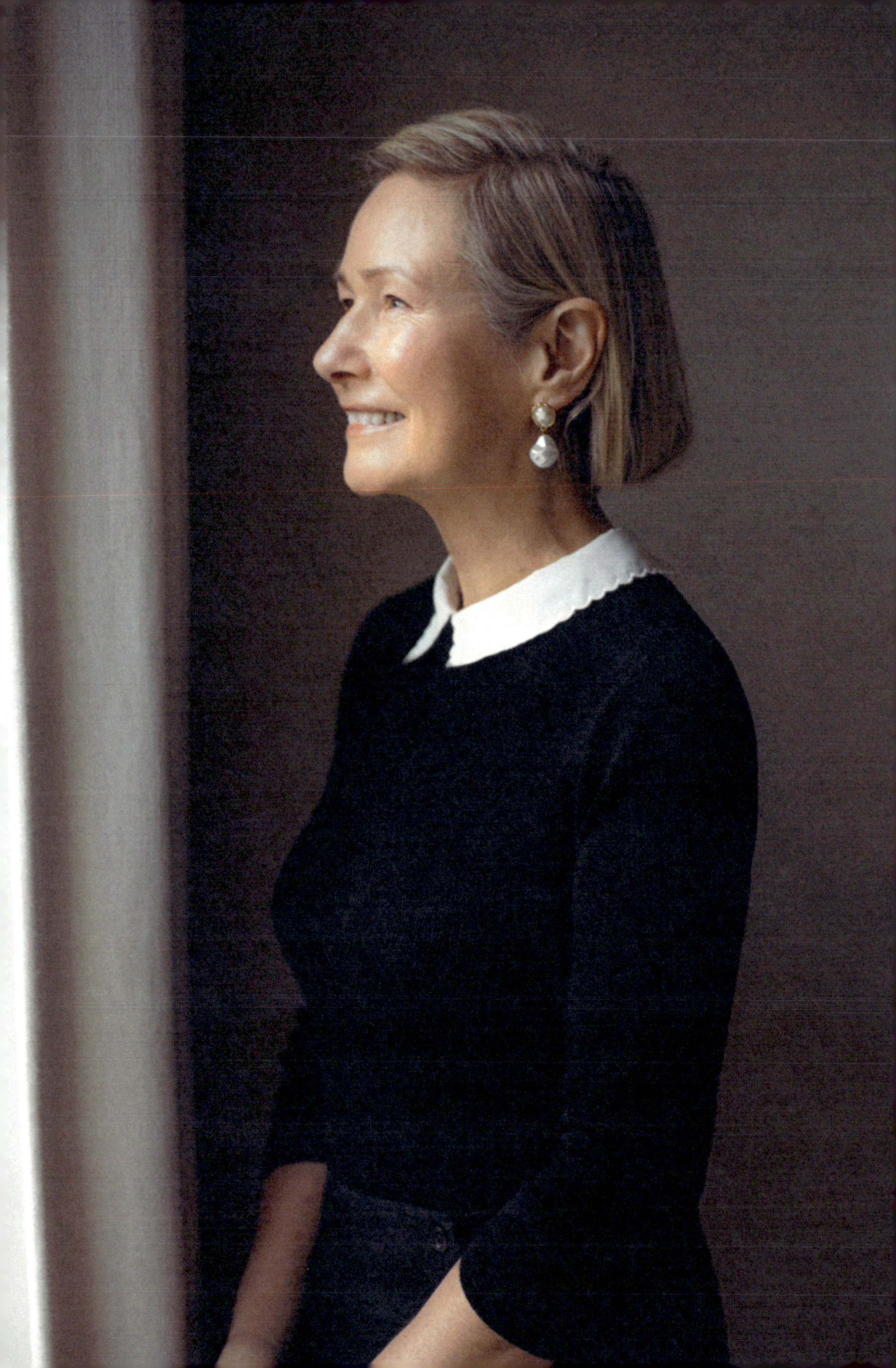

Heather talks

WORK AND PASSIONS

At 16, I started working and I worked until I was 71. Most of the time I worked in a bank. I also spent some time in a large company that had clothing stores all over the world. There I met a man 22 years younger than me, we lived together for ten years. In the end, I returned to the bank, and my 'toy boy' and I broke up.

The only time I didn't work was when I was in America. I volunteered at a school there. I was a storyteller and used to help children with their creative writing and their reading, and I used to read stories to them, introducing them to the English books that they hadn't heard before. First it was just my son's class I was reading to, and then I noticed that other teachers came in to listen and then I ended up reading to the whole school. It was fun and lovely.

I stopped working because my mother was very elderly and came to live with me. Also, they were closing lots of small branch banks, one of which was mine. I have not worked since – which I love! Now I see my friends, work in the garden, and just do what I want to do.

My best day at work? When you could wear whatever, you wanted in return for a donation to charity. No dress code! I was in pyjamas and huge slippers – that's how I worked in the bank all day, with a cup of tea, as if I was working from home.

Did I love my work? No. I think once you've started on the route, it's not easy to move to anything else. And you get more and more stuck in it. I liked working, but now I think I would have loved to have been an archaeologist instead. In my middle age, when I was working part time, I did a degree through the Open University. That opened my mind to the things I would like to have done if I'd done my degree earlier. Probably I would have been an archaeologist exploring wonderful sites in Turkey, Egypt, Peru... I saw a lot as a tourist, but how interesting it would have been to dive deeper.

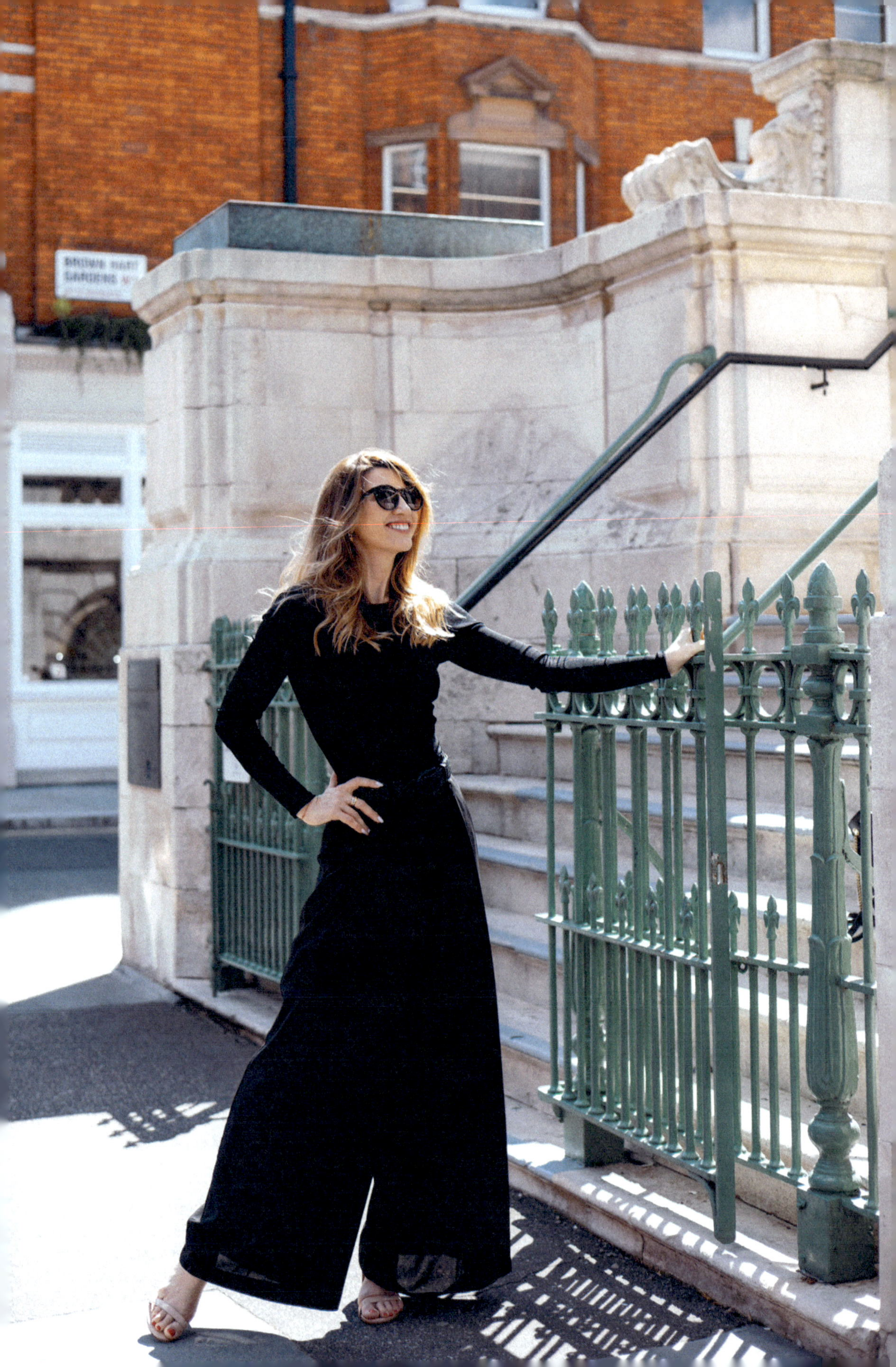

Did you know that...

British schools take uniforms very seriously. Basic items can be bought in almost any supermarket: dresses, skirts, pants, socks, knee socks and white shirts. Shoes are always black. Also, each school has a set of things in its own unique colours and with the school badge: blazers, jumpers, cardigans and sports uniforms. These must be bought in specialised stores. The school monitors the neat appearance of students and compliance with the school dress code. Although in high school girls roll up their skirts to the point that they are barely visible!

I like this tradition for several reasons. You don't have to think about what to dress your child in each day and the uniform is always cheaper than regular clothes. When everyone looks the same, there is no bullying because of who is wearing what. Convenient, cheap and psychologically more comfortable.

But once every two to four months, children can buy for £1 *(which goes to a chosen charity)* the opportunity to come to school dressed in whatever they want. You can come with green hair or in a princess dress. By the way, on such days, teachers are no less inventive in their looks.

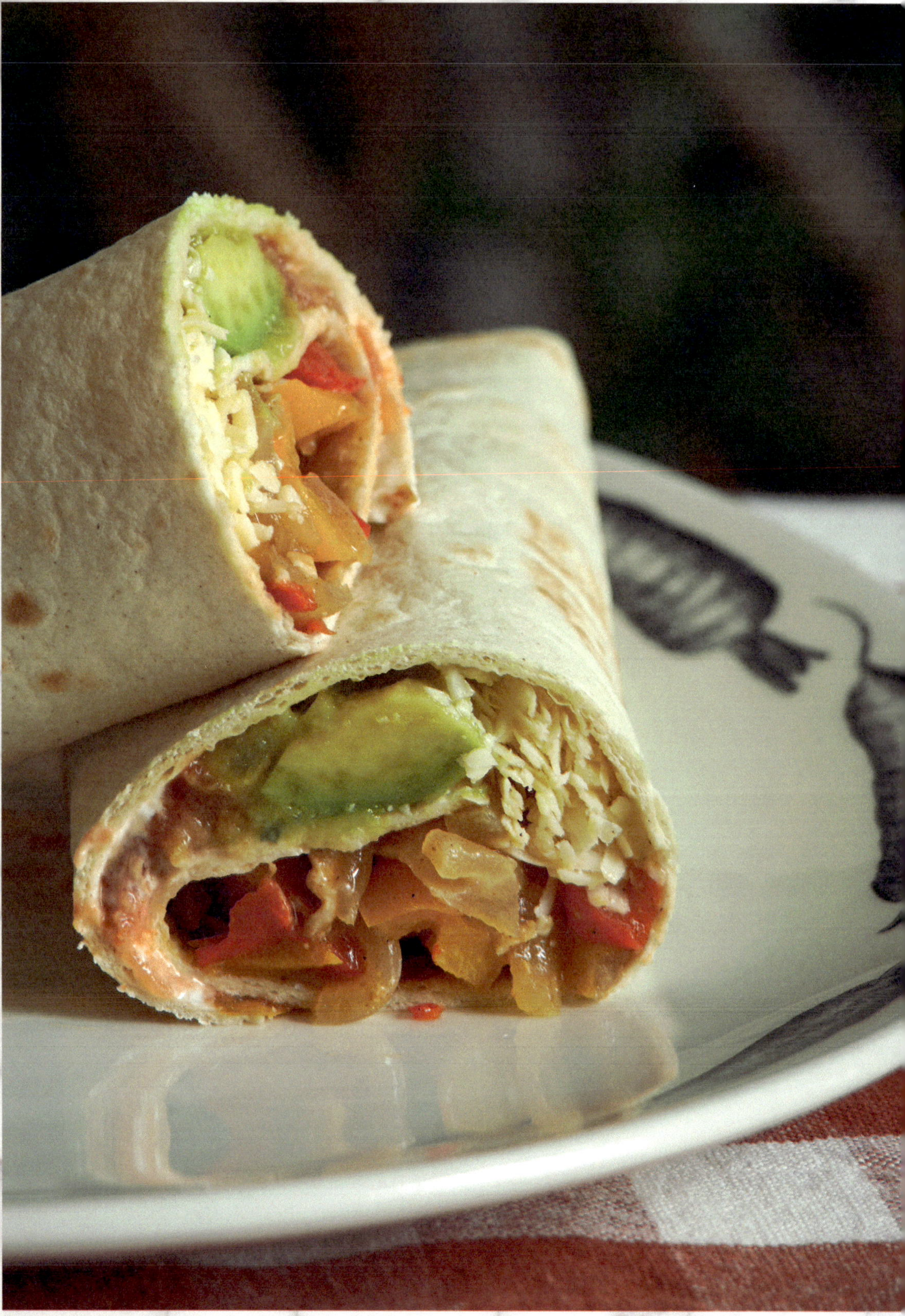

DINNER 5

Fajitas

Heather loves Mexican food.
We even had a week designated to it as a theme –
every day she cooked a new Mexican meal.

SERVES 4

500 g chicken *(or prawns, or Quorn pieces – whichever you prefer).*
Pack of flour tortillas *(large size)* allow 2-3 per person
Oil
1 red pepper
1 green pepper
1 onion

SEASONING MIX

1 tbsp cornflour
2 tsp chilli powder
1 tsp salt
1 tsp ground paprika
1 tsp white sugar
½ tsp onion powder
½ tsp garlic powder
½ tsp ground cumin
¼ tsp cayenne pepper

TOPPINGS

Sour cream
Grated cheddar cheese
Guacamole
1 jar of salsa
(thick and chunky)

1. Slice the chicken, peppers and onion into thin strips.
2. Pan fry the chicken in a little oil until thoroughly cooked.
3. Then, fry the peppers and onion over a medium-high heat until just beginning to soften.
4. Add the chicken to the vegetables and add the seasoning mix. Sizzle for about 5 minutes until the flavours are blended.
5. Heat the tortillas according to the pack.
6. Serve with toppings.

---

*If you want to use a ready-made packet of fajita seasoning mix that's fine too.
It works just as well and we are all for an easy life.*

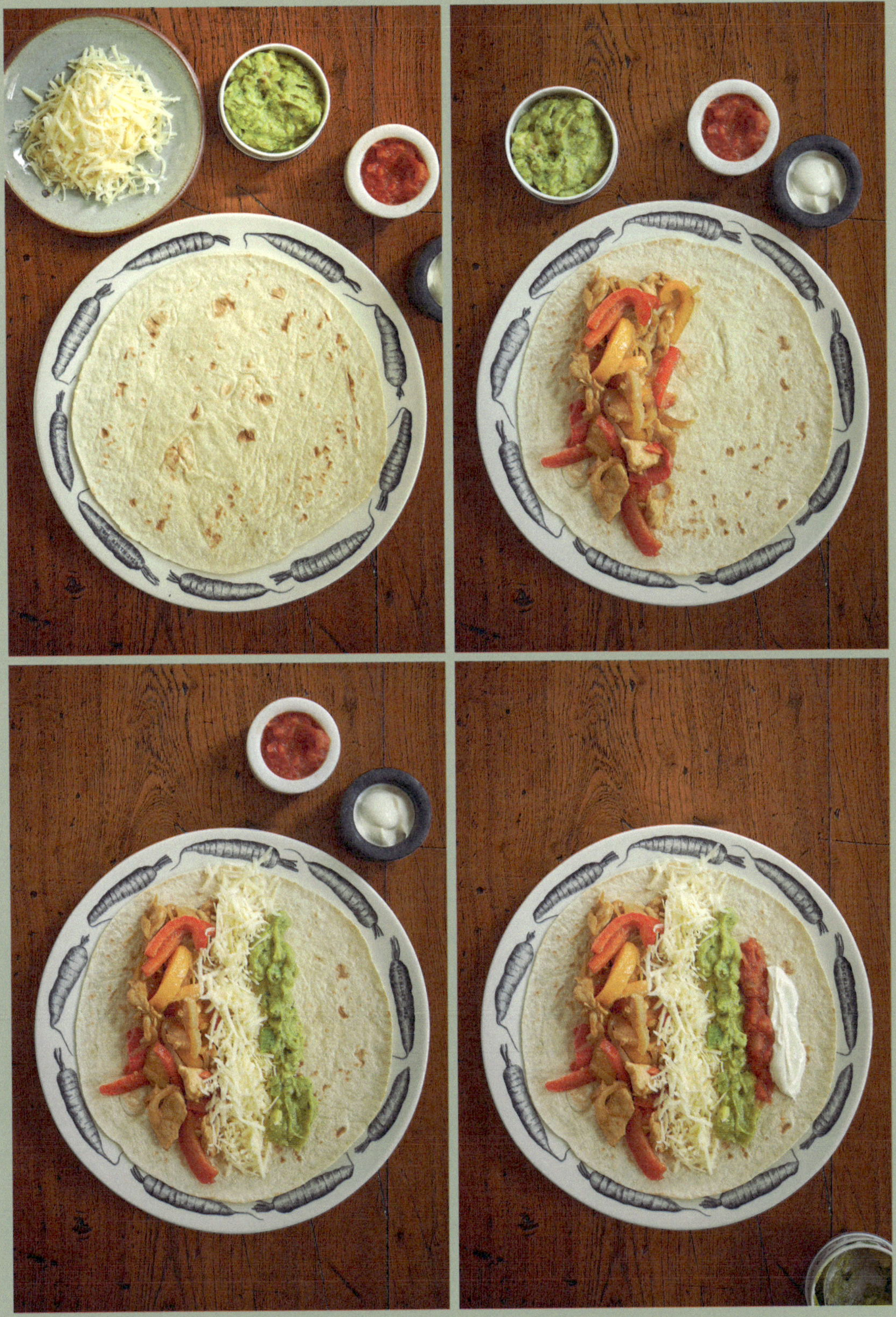

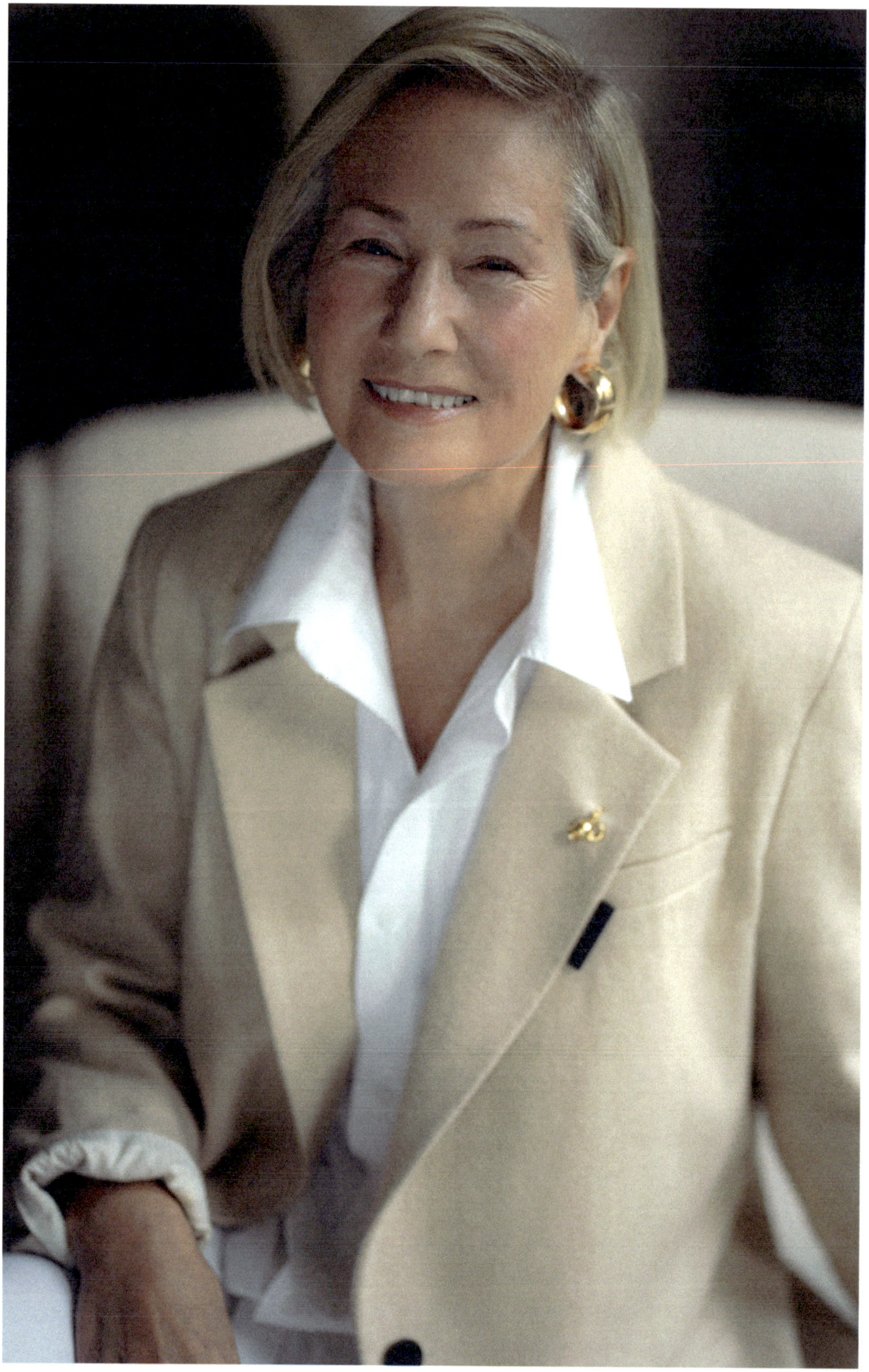

Heather talks

LIVING IN AMERICA

I brought my love for Mexican food from America. I was married to an American. He worked for the Pentagon and we lived south of Washington, D.C. for 3 years.

The big thing was the weather *(the British love talking about the weather!)* because they had real seasons. In winter it was cold and snowy. In the summer it was hot and sunny, we could plan a barbecue for six weeks in advance because we knew what the weather would be like. It's hard to imagine that in England, where it can rain at any moment.

I remember driving in America the first time. I was absolutely terrified. In the USA they drive on the right, as opposed to how we drive in the UK. I grabbed the steering wheel, my back dripping with sweat.

My shopping took me hours because I didn't recognize any of the food. Even cuts of meat look different and you don't know what you are supposed to do with them. I remember having long conversations with the butchers at the supermarket. It was a learning curve but it was enjoyable.

I loved the people in America – they work really hard, but they play hard too. I liked the lifestyle. We had a nice house that backed onto a lake where we could take out our canoe. There were beaver lodges, eagles, turtles... That was a nice experience, very different from England.

My husband liked to run and competed in marathons. I went to aerobic classes, volunteered at a school, and took care of the house and children. My stepson was 15 and my son was 7. Unfortunately, my stepson died very young. I look back at those days when the boys were together and it was just one of those good times in life. You don't ever appreciate when everything is right until it isn't, do you?

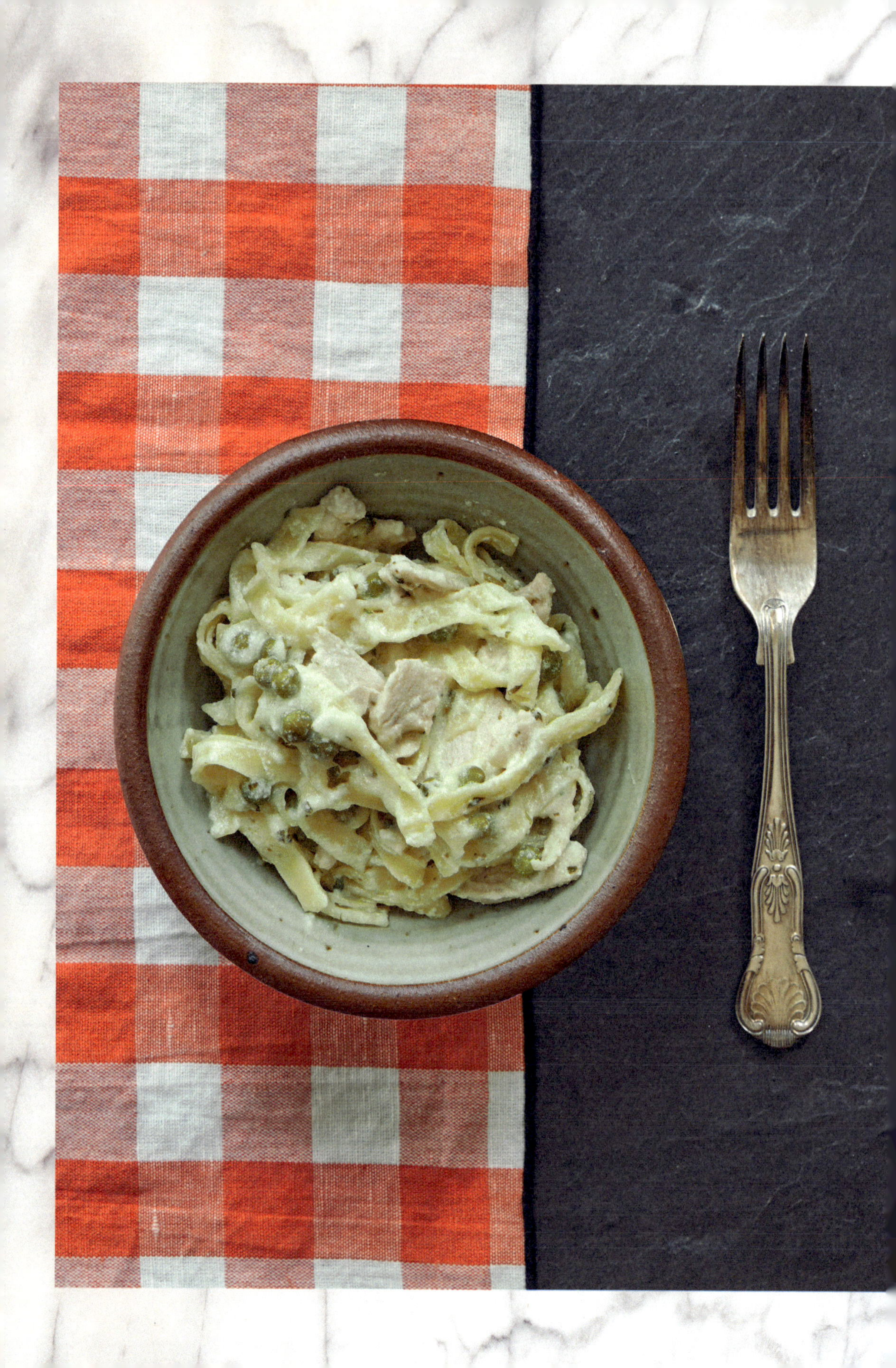

DINNER 6

Lemon Chicken Pasta

Heather loves making pasta because it's quick and easy. She usually serves this light, lemony version with a green salad dressed with French dressing. A great summer lunch or dinner any time of the year!

500 g farfalle or tagliatelle pasta
500 g chicken breast fillets, sliced into 1 cm slices
150 g frozen peas, defrosted
180 ml chicken stock
125 g ricotta
60 ml lemon juice
1 clove of garlic, crushed
1 tbsp olive oil
1 tbsp cornflour
1 tbsp basil leaves, chopped
1 tbsp parsley leaves, chopped
½ tsp lemon rind, grated

1. Cook the pasta uncovered in boiling water until al dente and drain.
2. Meanwhile, heat the oil and fry the chicken until tender, then remove from the pan.
3. Add the remaining ingredients to the pan and heat until the mixture boils and thickens, then return the chicken and add the cooked pasta.

Heather sometimes substitutes the chicken with smoked haddock poached in milk, using the milk instead of the chicken stock for the sauce. Also, if you don't have ricotta, 3 tablespoons of crème fraîche or 125 ml of cream work well too.

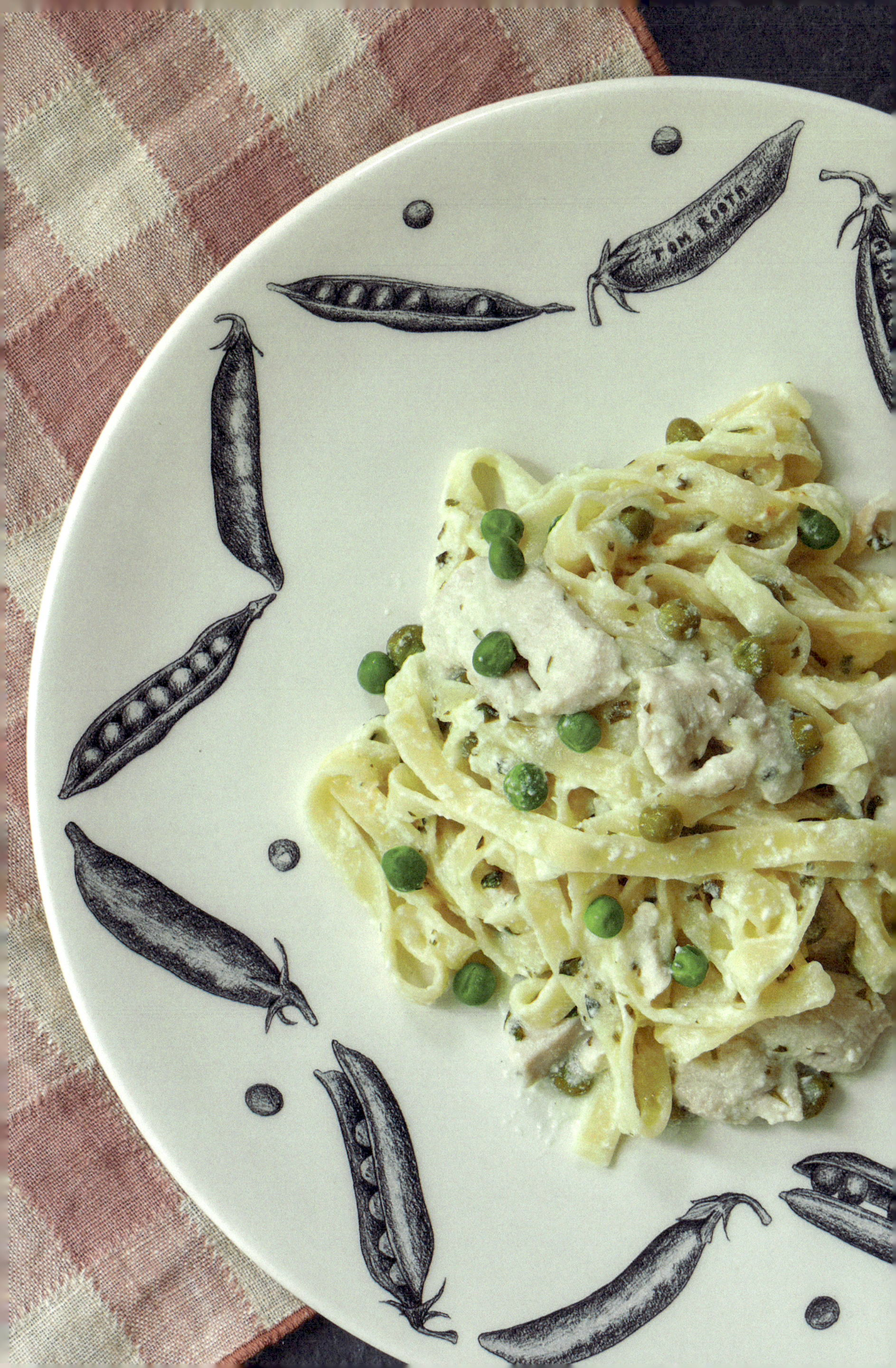
TOM BOOTH

" *I make myself* LUNCH OR DINNER *every day,* DESPITE THE SUPERMARKETS FULL OF PREPARED FOOD. I THINK IT'S *very easy to slip into 'junk food'* MODE.

Heather talks

COOKING AS A CHORE AND INSPIRATION

Honestly, I'm not a great fan of cooking. Occasionally, if I've got time and want to try something new, then I cook. It's all right. But I think if I had all that time back that I've spent shopping for food, preparing food, cooking food, clearing up after the food – it would be half my life!

I think cooking for women, especially for women who work as I did until quite recently, is just another chore at the end of the day. Men are different. They cook for relaxation, as something creative after their working life. When I cooked it was feeding a family. I've done a day's work, I've still got laundry to do and things to get ready for school – oh and what am I going to cook for dinner? It's your job to feed your family healthily and that's what you do. Not fun, eh? I'd rather go out in the sunshine, do gardening, or do anything else other than cooking. Anita, you are so naughty that you made me do all these recipes!

Why do I cook lunch or dinner for myself every day, when supermarkets are full of ready-made food, or I can just quickly grab something on the go? Well, for example, recently I had such a day: I ate some nuts, then crackers, then pizza, and in the end I felt bad. It's very easy to slip into this junk-food mode. But this does not happen when there is a habit of cooking fresh food. It helps me stay healthy and feel good, physically and mentally. Perhaps, this is what inspires me to cook for myself, set the table, choose sauces and seasonings.

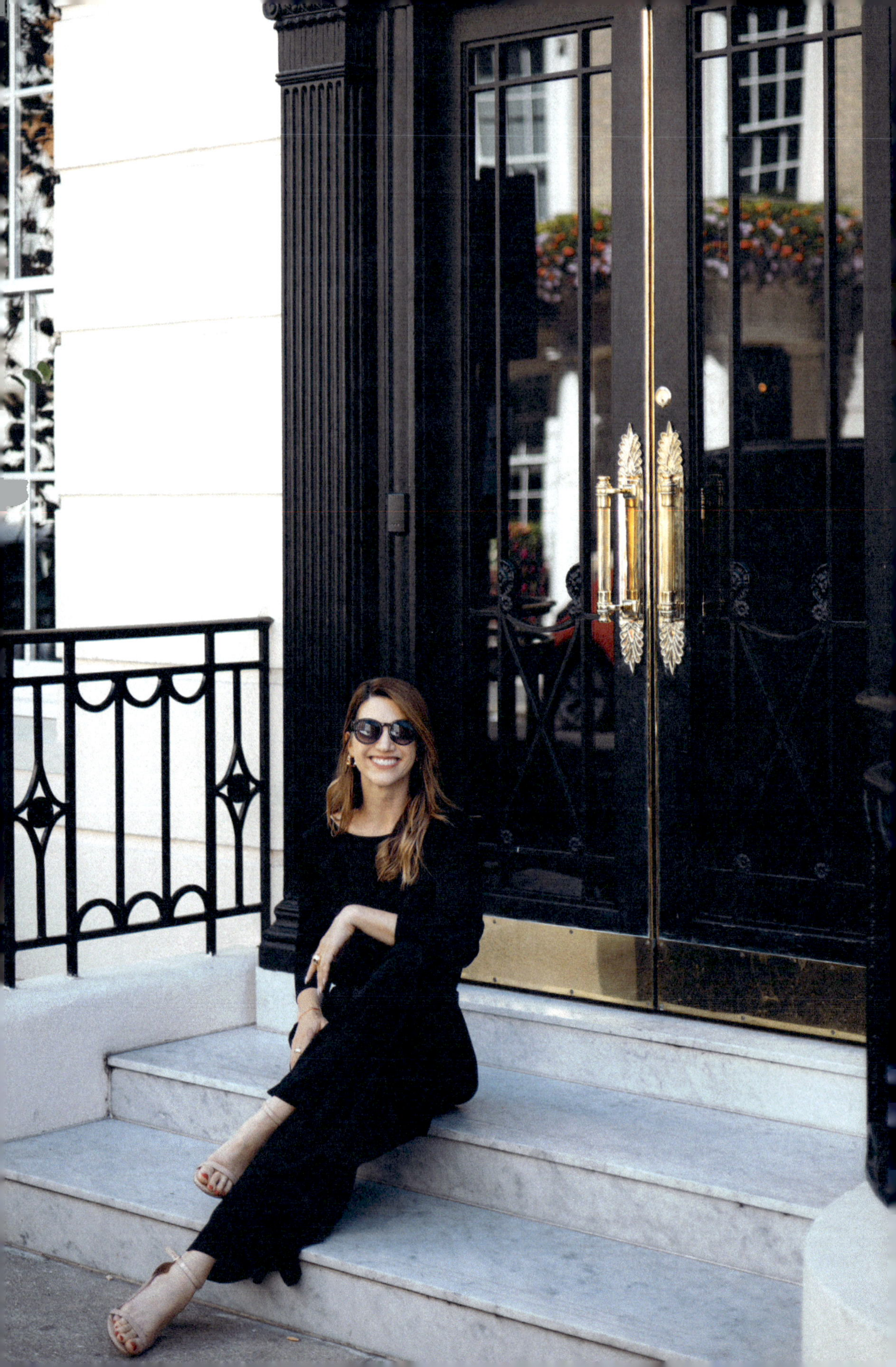

In Great Britain, houses often have names instead
of numbers – for example The Willows, Corner House, Cook's Farm.
It's cute, but it greatly reduces your chances
of finding the right house!

Did you know that...

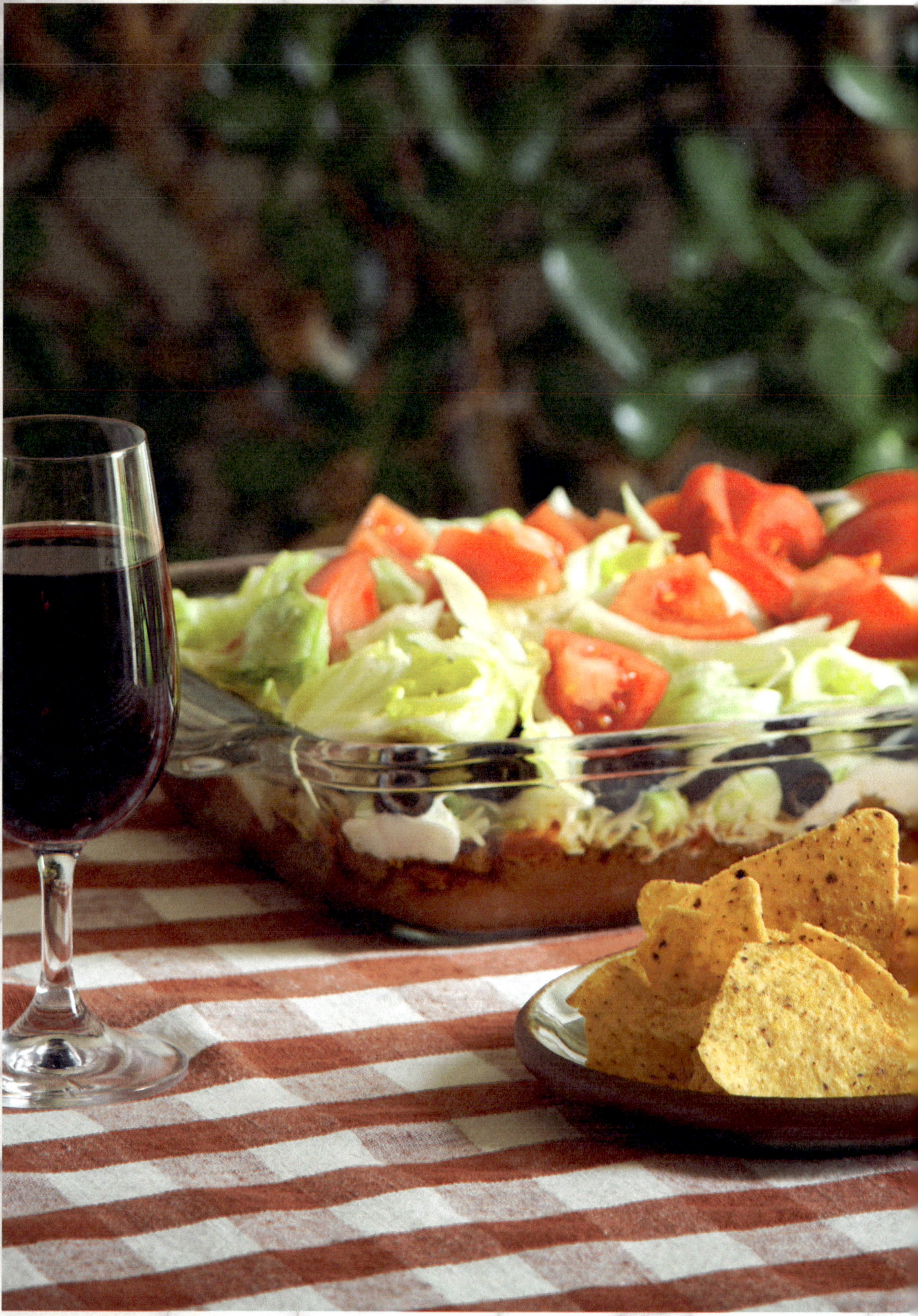

DINNER
7

Super Taco Salad

This recipe was given to Heather by a Mexican friend when she went to live in America about 40 years ago and it has been a family favourite ever since. The best thing about this salad is that it can be eaten any time from hot to cold the next day.

SERVES 4-6

In a 23 x 33 cm baking dish layer:

Layer 1. 1 can (435 g) of refried beans. If these are not available, make it yourself according to the recipe on the next page.

Layer 2. 450 g of minced beef, browned, drained, and seasoned with cumin and garlic salt.

Layer 3. 2 small cans of chopped green chilies or jalapenos, drained. Take care, they are very spicy. Just add to your own taste.

Layer 4. 226 g jar of taco sauce or any variety of salsa *(mild or hot)*.

Layer 5. 650 g grated cheddar cheese, or enough to cover the other ingredients in an even layer.

Bake in the oven at 200°C (180°C fan) until the cheese is bubbly. Remove from the oven and let cool slightly then sprinkle evenly over the top:

Layer 6. 25 g spring onions, chopped.

Layer 7. 250 g sour cream.

Layer 8. 180 g sliced black olives.

Layer 9. 100 g chopped tomatoes.

Layer 10. 40 g chopped lettuce.

Layer 11. 220 g grated cheddar cheese.

The meat layer can be substituted with vegetarian mince and the sour cream with guacamole.

> Note that the bottom five layers are cooked in the oven, and the next six are laid out ready on top.

HOW TO MAKE REFRIED BEANS

2 x 425 g can of pinto beans, drained
2 tbsp rapeseed oil
2 garlic cloves, peeled
Juice of ½ lime
1 tsp cumin
1 tsp chilli powder
Salt to taste

Heat the oil in a heavy pan over a medium heat and cook the garlic cloves for 4-5 minutes until brown on both sides, then mash them with a fork. Add the beans, spices and salt to the pan and heat for about 5 minutes, stirring occasionally. Mash the mixture with a potato masher. Squeeze the lime juice over and stir until combined.

Did you know that...

A traditional English breakfast is a huge pile of food. It includes fried eggs, bacon, sausages, black pudding, tomatoes, mushrooms, baked beans and toast. For those who don't have enough, they can also add hash browns. Wash it down with tea. But first add milk to it!

Heather talks

COFFEE FOR BREAKFAST AND HER HEALTH

My grandmother was old fashioned. She believed in breakfast being the most important meal of the day. A big breakfast. But as a child I could never eat it. I wasn't ready to eat so early in the morning, it used to give me stomach cramps. I just didn't want it. So, when I became a grown-up, I decided: I don't have to eat when I am not hungry. And since the age of 16, when I left home, I have never eaten breakfast.

I think we don't need to eat more than twice a day. Although each person is different. Some people like to eat their breakfast in the morning and then they might go without lunch.

I cannot start the day without a cup of black coffee. That's my treat in the morning.

I get hungry between 12 and 1 p.m., and I eat my lunch. By then I've been fasting for quite a long time from the night before, so I usually have a bagel or a sandwich. Lunch is my carb time. Or sometimes I just have a salad or a soup. There's always some homemade soup in the freezer. Lentil, parsnip, and vegetable soups are my favourites.

As for dinner, it's protein and vegetables for me. If I have lunch somewhere, in a pub or cafe, I try to make dinner light *(for example, I eat hummus with vegetables or a small portion of crisps with cheese)*, or just skip it completely. If I had a sandwich for lunch, expect a hearty dinner with lots of cheese *(I love cheddar)*. And, of course, wine! I believe that one or two glasses of Malbec in the evening can only be beneficial!

I must say that I am ridiculously healthy. I am never ill, and I never take medicines. I don't think I've ever had a headache. I must be doing something right for my body. It works for me and you have to find what works for you. Listen to your own body and decide what's good for it.

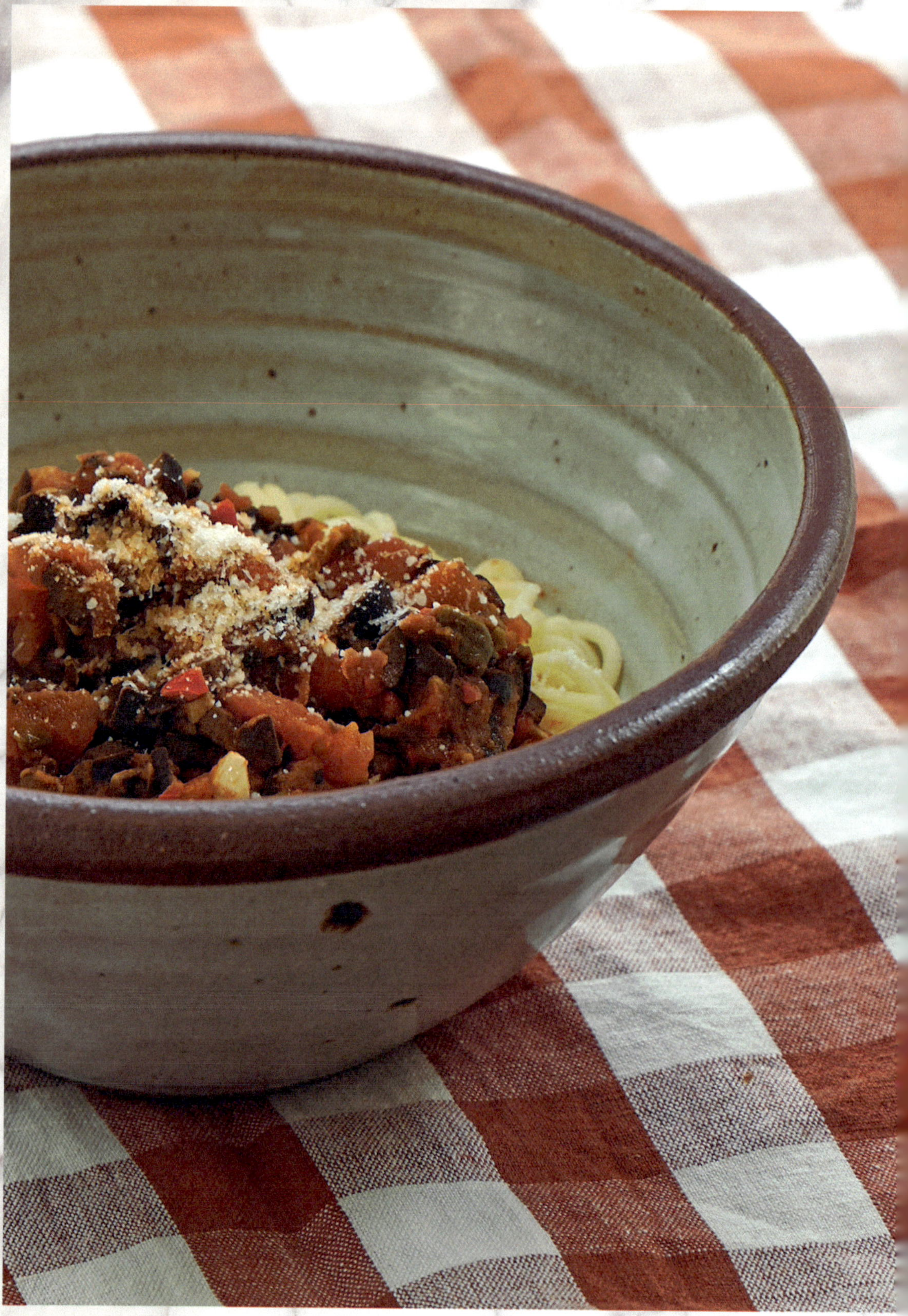

DINNER

8

Pasta Puttanesca

The name of this spicy Neapolitan dish translates as 'whore's pasta'. According to legend, during the day, when shops and markets were open the ladies of the night slept, and when they woke up, they prepared breakfast from what was in the household pantry. Quick, nutritious, tasty and spicy – everything Heather and I like.

SERVES 4

Whole Wheat spaghetti
(enough for 4 people)
A drizzle of olive oil

THE SAUCE

3 cloves of garlic
2 x 400 g tins of peeled plum tomatoes
170 g sliced pitted black olives, drained and chopped
2 x 50 g tins of anchovies, drained and chopped
2 red chillies, deseeded and chopped or 1 tsp crushed chilli flakes
4 tbsp olive oil
2 tbsp capers, drained
2 tbsp tomato puree
2 tbsp chopped fresh basil
Pepper to taste

TO SERVE

Grated parmesan

1. To make the sauce, heat the oil and gently cook the garlic, chilli, and basil until the garlic is soft and golden *(1-2 minutes)*. Then add the rest of the ingredients and simmer uncovered for about 30 minutes until the sauce is thick and the liquid has evaporated.
2. In the meantime, cook the pasta in boiling water with a drizzle of olive oil to prevent it from sticking together. When the pasta is 'al dente', drain it, top with the sauce and serve with grated parmesan.

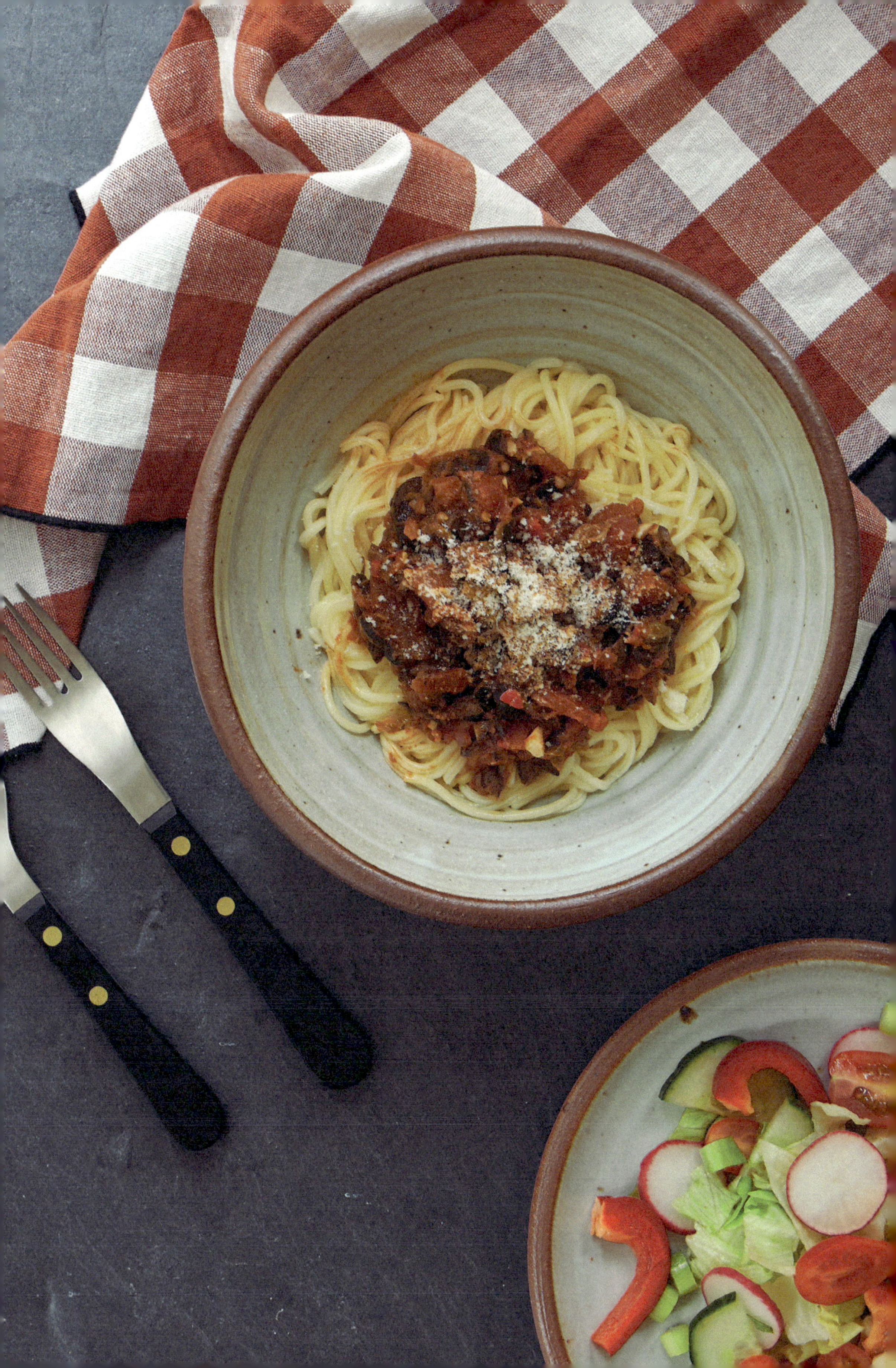

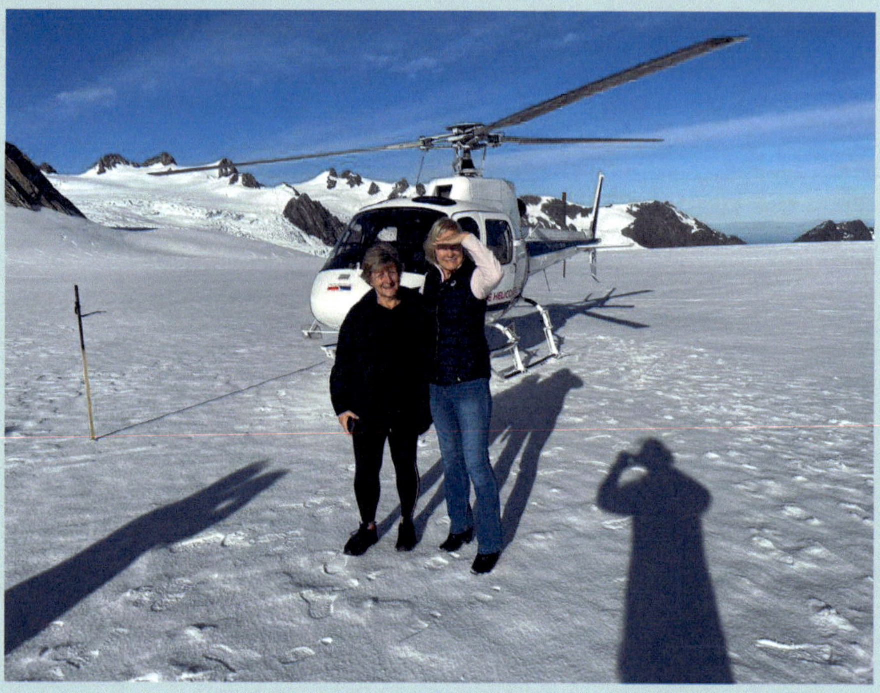

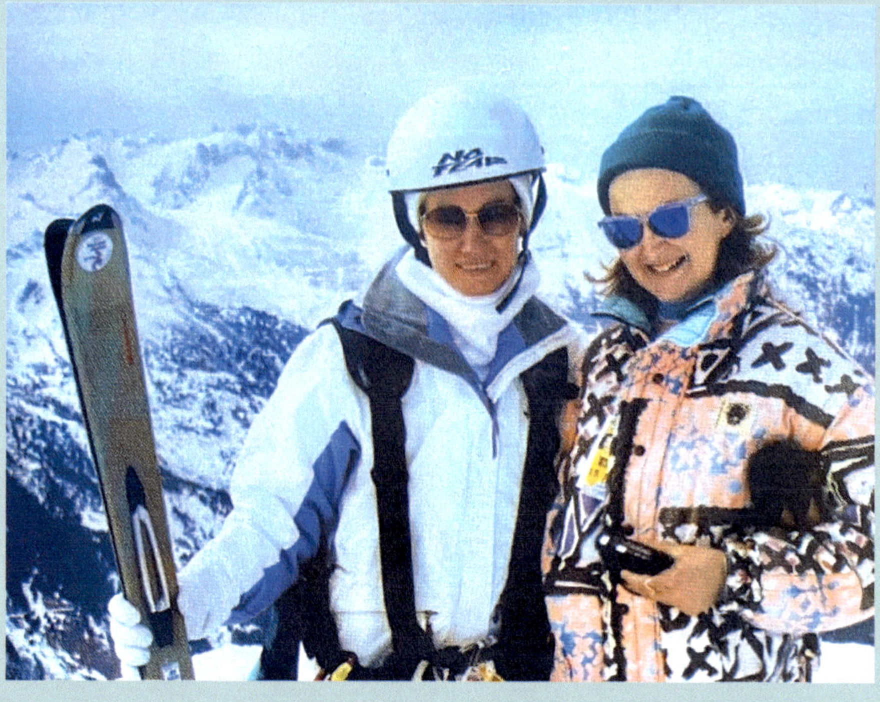

Heather talks

TRAVELLING TO THE ENDS OF THE WORLD

I've always liked to travel. When I was married to my American husband, we got stuck in a routine. We would go skiing in the winter in Europe, and in the summer we would go home to see his family at the lakes in New Hampshire. We didn't really do anything else; it was always the same.

So, after I divorced him, I travelled to places where I wanted to go. Ever since then I've travelled all around the world. I've been to Japan, Peru and India amongst other places. It is always somewhere new because the world is such a big, beautiful place. I want to see as much of it as I can. My idea is that I go as far as I can while I can physically still do that. When I get older, perhaps less able to do long flights, then I'll stay nearer to home.

So, I am going to New Zealand next year with a friend I used to work with. We booked a 4-week tour of New Zealand, and then we're going to Fiji for a week. Next on my list is Canada: different culture, magnificent scenery.

I was always thinking of something further than Europe. I knew nothing about Ukraine until this war happened. The only thing I'd seen on the news there were these beautiful golden domes in Kyiv. You told me so many interesting things about Ukraine and I definitely will go and see you there. You'll show me everything, we'll eat syrnyki – as I know, Ukrainians adore them. By the way, I liked them too, although this is an unusual taste for the British. And how delicious your borscht is!

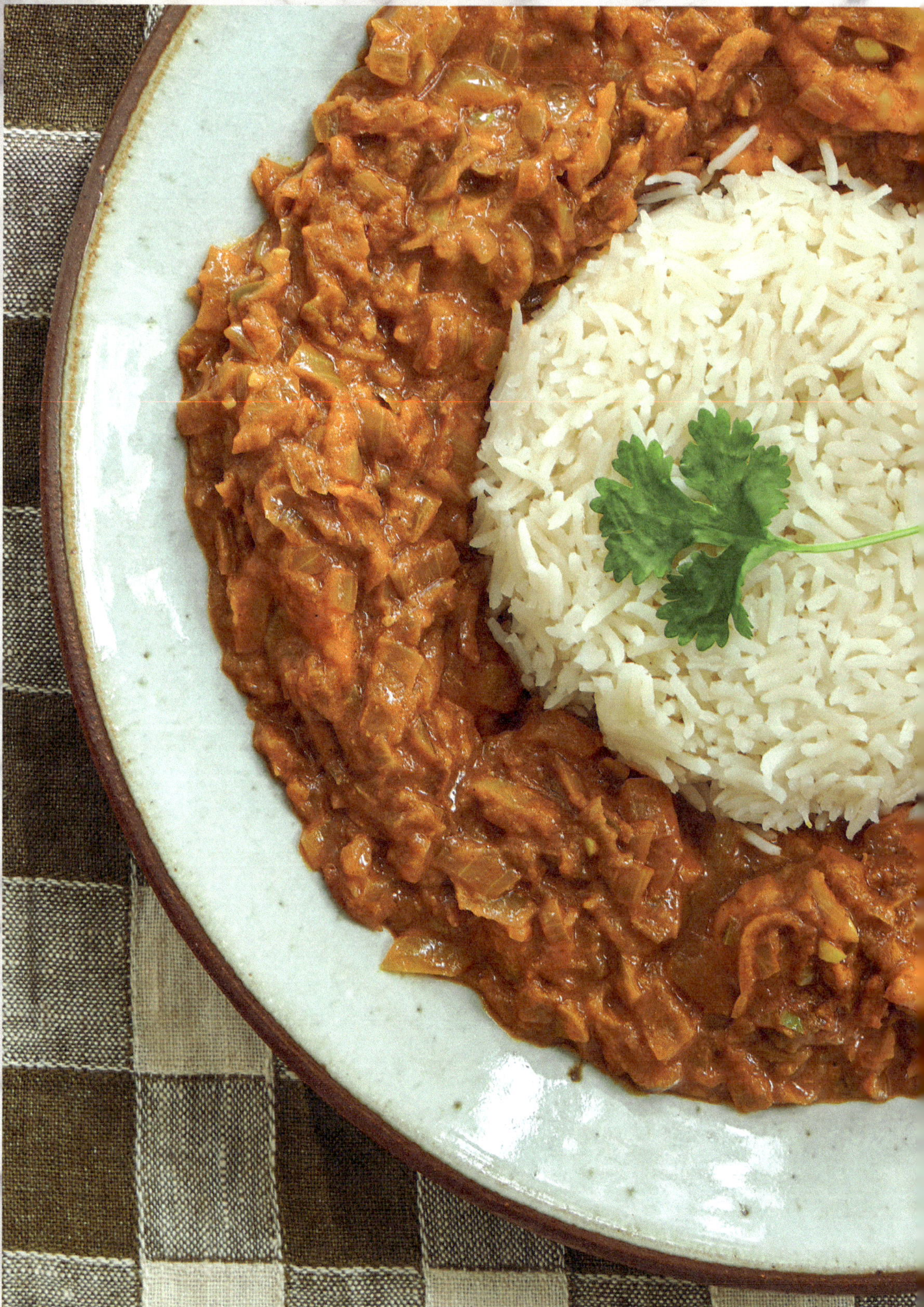

DINNER

9

Prawn Curry

This dish is made by Heather using a recipe from her cousin. He is now retired and has lived predominantly in Germany for most of his adult life, but he spent a year of his youth in Southern India, hence his love of a good curry.

SERVES 2

1 can of coconut milk or coconut cream

12 medium – large raw prawns, shelled and deveined

2-3 medium tomatoes, skinned and chopped

2 medium onions, chopped or thinly sliced

2 cloves of garlic, crushed

1 green chilli, chopped

2-3 dessert spoons of peanut oil

2 tsp tomato puree

1 heaped tsp freshly grated ginger

1 tsp turmeric powder

1 tsp cumin powder

1 tsp brown sugar

1 tsp tamarind pulp

½ tsp chilli powder

½ tsp coriander powder

½ tsp garam masala

Salt to taste

Fresh coriander, finely chopped

1. Heat the oil and fry the onions until translucent. Add the sugar and slightly caramelise, then add the tomato puree. Next, add the green chilli and turmeric, then the chilli powder, cumin, coriander and garam masala. After 1-2 minutes add the tomatoes, garlic, and ginger.
2. Simmer for about 5 minutes *(to allow the flavours to infuse)* before adding the coconut cream, tamarind pulp, and salt to taste.
3. After a further 5 minutes add the prawns and simmer slowly until the prawns turn pink/red. Do not overcook or boil as this will spoil the delicate flavour of the prawns and make them tough.
4. Turn off the heat and add some fresh chopped coriander to taste.
5. Serve with basmati rice.

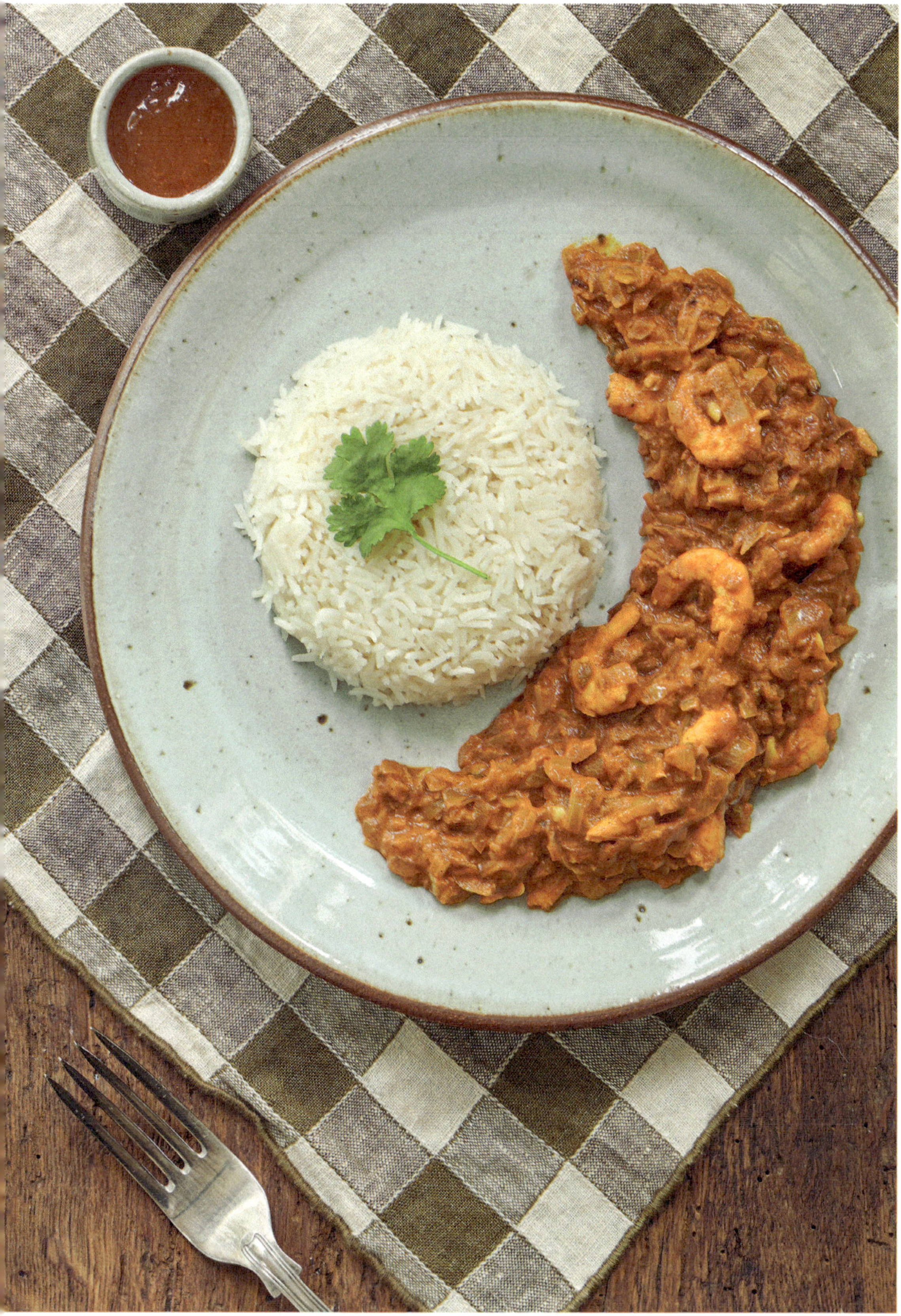

Heather talks

EXTREME HOBBIES

I was aways into some active sports – Latin American dances, ice skating, skiing, rollerblading, hang gliding or horse riding. When I had my son, I put everything on hold, but when he grew up, I started again to do what I love.

During my life, I've done a parachute jump, walked on the wing of an aeroplane, rolled down a slope inside a transparent ball *(this is called zorbing!)*, gone rock climbing, flown a paraglider – I guess I've tried everything possible. My stepson was a surfer, so I also got on a board in the ocean. Now, I continue to roller-skate along the sea front.

I've done most of it in the UK. Because when I'm travelling, I'm more into seeing other cultures and things like that. Although I did do paraskiing in Austria: it's when you ski off the edge of a mountain with a parachute – it's just amazing!

I was very fond of horse riding. But then the friend I did it with died of breast cancer, so I stopped doing this because it wasn't the same without her. Although I still want to learn to ride like a real lady – side-saddle. Thank you for reminding me, I will add it to my to-do list.

I think skydiving was the most extreme one. It was fun, I would do it again, it's quite expensive though. At least I've done that and now I have these memories.

The one I want to try next is JetLeving. You haven't heard of this? You wear a backpack which works as a water pressure device and allows you to skim across the water surface or shoot up into the air. It's like flying over the water!

Why do I do this? If you work in a bank most of your life you need something to make life exciting. But I think I just enjoy the adrenaline. Life is very short and we never know when our last day comes. It's such a big world and so much to see and do. I want to get as much from it as I can.

> **"**
> I LOVE FEELING *adrenaline.* OUR LIFE IS SHORT, AND *the world is so big,* IT HAS SO MUCH TO SEE AND DO. SO I *want to get the most out of it!*

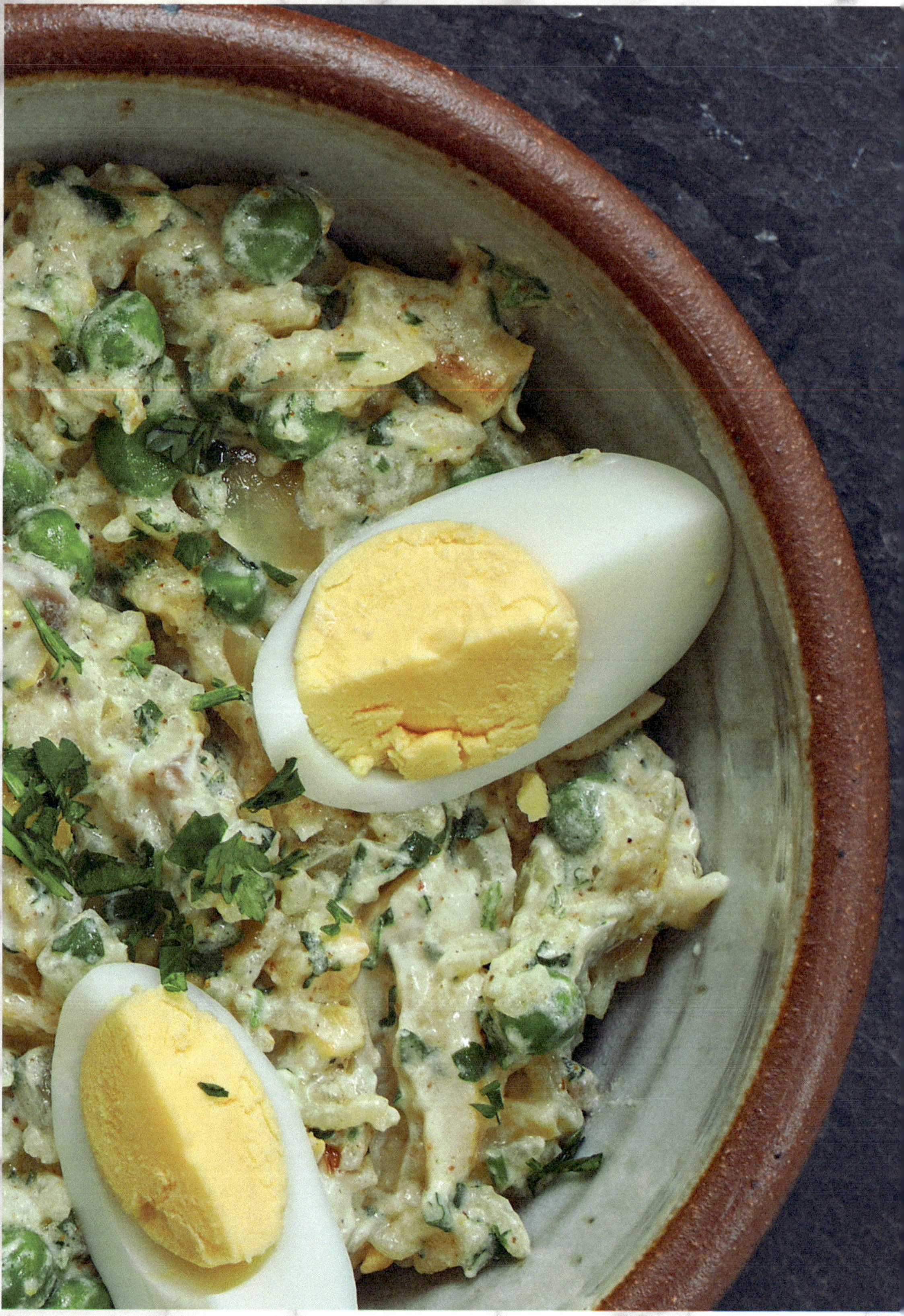

DINNER
10

Smoked Haddock Kedgeree

This dish, beloved by the British, originates from the Indian dish khichuri, which can be traced back to 1340. It is often eaten for breakfast in England, but is equally good for lunch or dinner.

SERVES 4

400 g smoked haddock
250 g long grain rice
200 ml creme fraiche
200 g frozen peas
2 large eggs
4 tsp medium Madras curry powder
1 medium onion, chopped
1 red pepper, diced
2 tsp Dijon mustard
1 tbsp oil
1 clove of garlic
25 g parsley, chopped
Salt to taste

1. Cook the rice with one teaspoon of curry powder in boiling water for 12-15 minutes until tender and then drain.
2. Boil the eggs for 10 mins, peel and cut into quarters.
3. Poach the haddock in boiling water for 3-4 minutes, then drain, remove the skin and any pin bones, flake and set aside.
4. Heat the oil in a large frying pan and fry the onion, garlic and pepper until soft. Add the remaining curry powder, rice and peas and heat through.
5. Finally, stir in the parsley, creme fraiche, mustard and fish.
6. Serve topped with the boiled eggs.

Heather likes her food hot, but it gets cold quickly on the plate. Therefore, before serving, she always heats the plates in the microwave or in the oven. Heather says she once spied this trick at a restaurant and has been doing it ever since.

> *make-up* IS SOMETHING I'VE NEVER LOVED. PROBABLY BECAUSE *i don't know how to put* IT ON.

Heather talks

HIGH HEELS AND BEAUTY ROUTINE

I worked in an office where I have always had to dress smartly. So, my style is classic. I have always loved high heels. They make your legs look longer. I just like that look and I don't see why I should stop doing it just because I'm ancient now! I remember your face seeing all my shoes at the bottom of the stairs when I was going out one night. You couldn't believe I was wearing heels that high! Ankle boots, sandals with 10 cm heels and elegant pumps are still my favourites.

Still, I do have my days when I don't wear my heels. For example, when I am doing the garden, I can't wear them because they will destroy my beautiful lawn.

If I'm in complete harmony with heels, makeup is something I've never loved. I think it's because I have never learnt to use it properly. Every time I tried it when I was younger, I looked like a clown and I thought, 'No, I can't do that.'

It's funny that young girls nowadays wear so much makeup, such dark eyebrows, lots of foundation. I think, 'That's the time of your life when your skin is beautiful, why cover it up?'

So, I have never worn makeup, but I do moisturise my skin every morning. Every time I have a shower, I put on my body cream and my face cream and serums and things like that. But nothing else. I use SPF 50 sun cream when I go to a hot country. In England? Phh, you can't really tell if it's summer or not half the time. However, UV protection and our climate protects us from skin cancer and keeps our skin younger for longer.

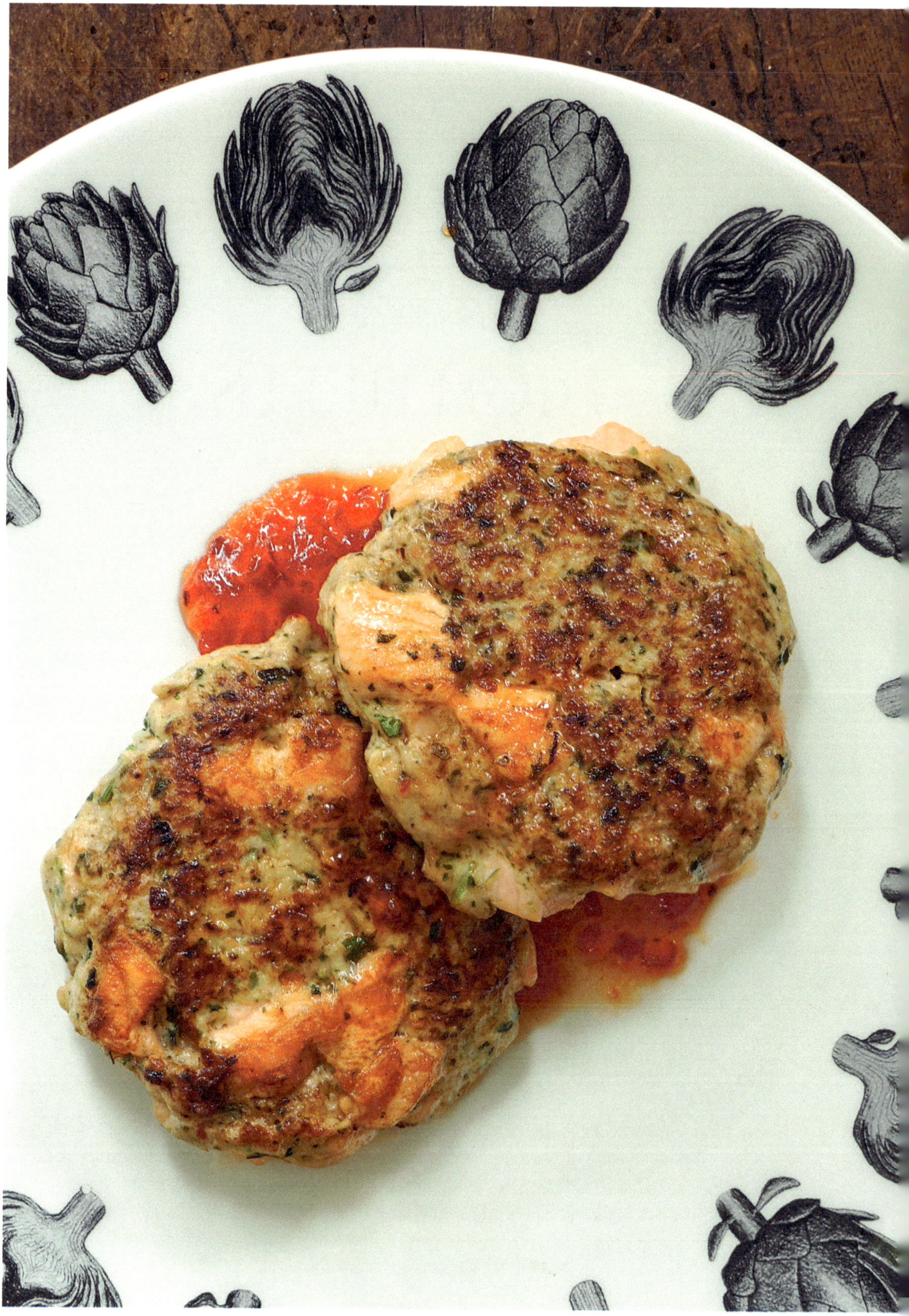

DINNER 11

Thai Fish Cakes

This is an ideal recipe for a light lunch for 4 people
or served with rice and steamed vegetables
as a dinner for 2.

SERVES 2-4

4 skinless and boneless salmon fillets (500 g)
2 tbsp fish sauce
2 tbsp vegetable oil
1 stick of lemongrass
1 tbsp Thai red curry paste
15 g coriander, finely chopped
2 spring onions, finely sliced
6 cm piece of ginger
1 tsp lime zest

1. Remove the tough outer layer of leaves on the lemongrass and peel the ginger. Chop very finely together or put into a food processor. Next, add two of the salmon fillets, lime zest, fish sauce, curry paste and coriander and process until blended into a smooth, mousse-like paste.
2. Chop the remaining salmon into 1 cm chunks and slice the spring onions, then mix both into the blended salmon paste. Divide the mixture into four and form into 2 cm thick patties.
3. Fry in a nonstick frying pan for about 3 minutes per side and serve with sweet chilli sauce or chilli jam and a rocket salad.

Ready prepared 'cheats', like ginger and lemongrass in tubes from the supermarket, save time and are handy to keep in the fridge.

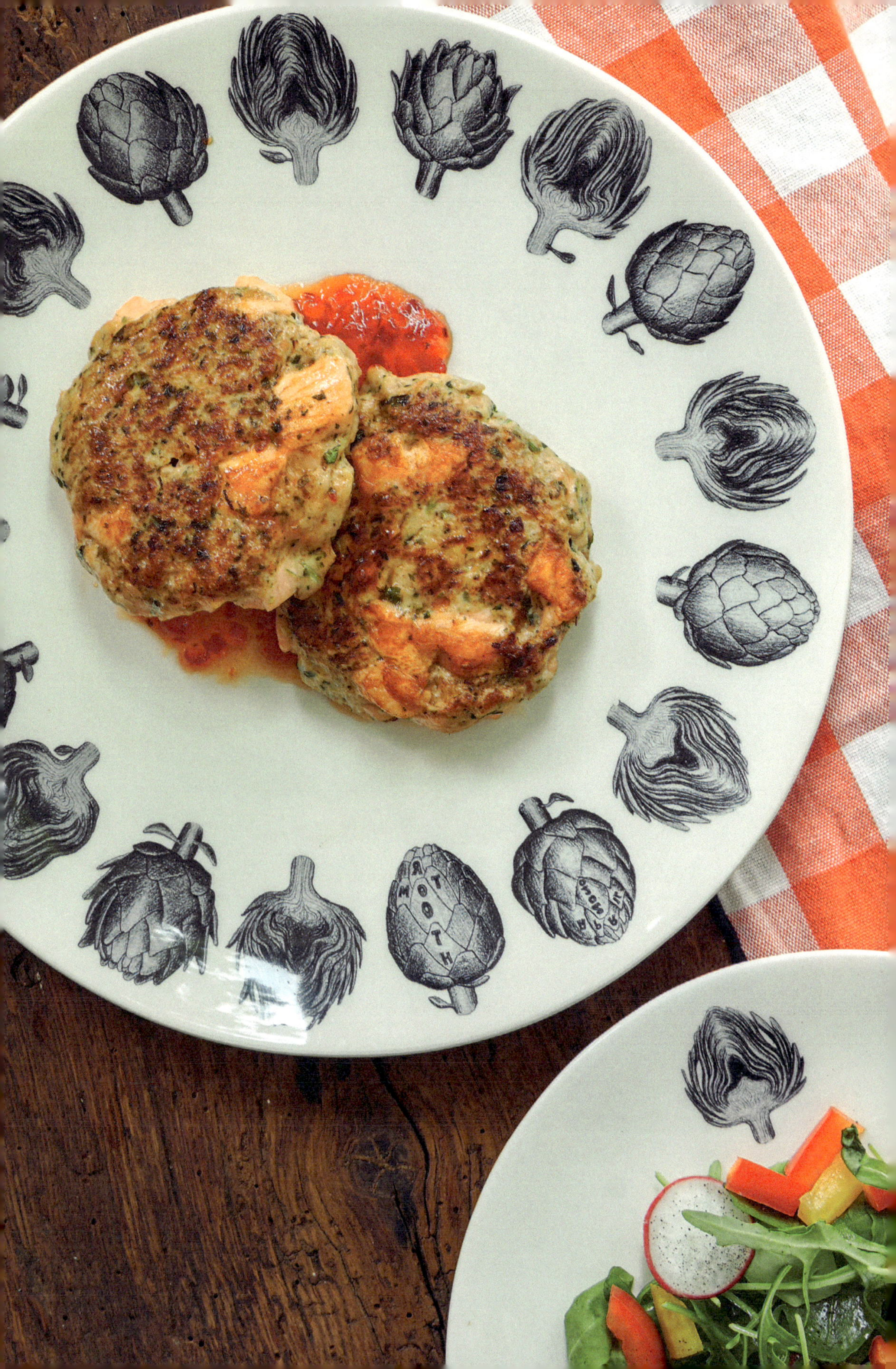

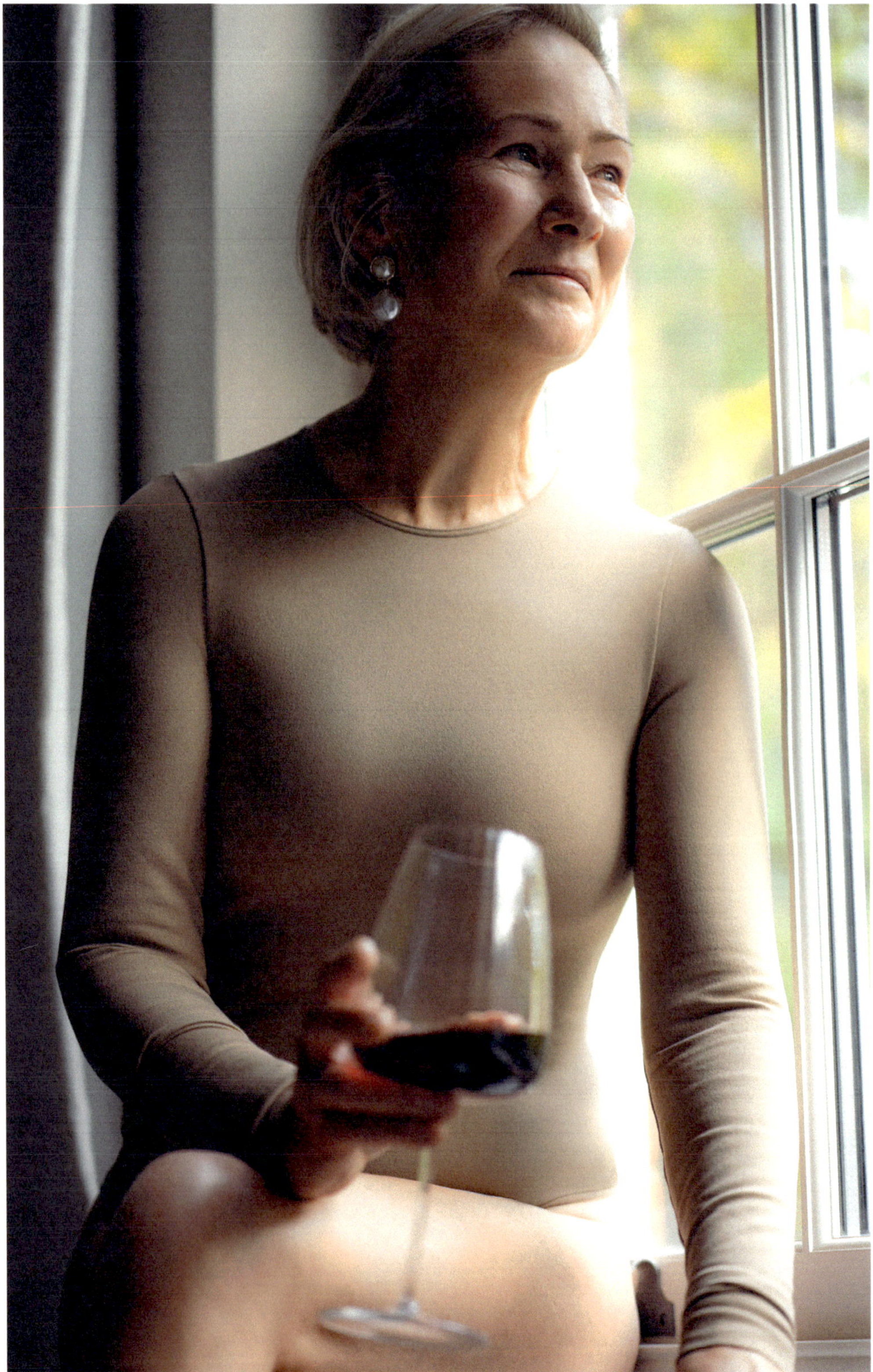

Heather talks

MEN, DATING AND RELATIONSHIPS

When I left my husband, I had a long-time affair with a man who was very much younger than me. That was nice for a while, but in the end, it doesn't work when you don't share the same sort of history.

I've done dating websites and things like that, but I don't think they work as well as just meeting someone in the normal way. It's difficult, and when you get older it gets progressively more difficult. I've always said to my friends that online dating is like a biscuit tin – there's only the broken bits left on the bottom of the tin when it gets to my age.

So, I've decided that it should be a normal course of events – when you meet someone through friends or at the pub and you can talk to them and get to know them, rather than those stilted online dating conversations and awkward meetings when you think, 'Oh god, really?!'.

Besides, I'd rather be alone than with someone I don't really like. There is such a problem that men don't look after themselves. They age badly. The big bellies and the grey beards? No, thanks.

What kind of men do I like? Men with grey hair, in rare sports cars, athletic and fit. I like bad guys more than good ones. Those who make me laugh, know how to give emotional gifts, be unpredictable, love spontaneous trips – these are the things that can keep me around for more than one season.

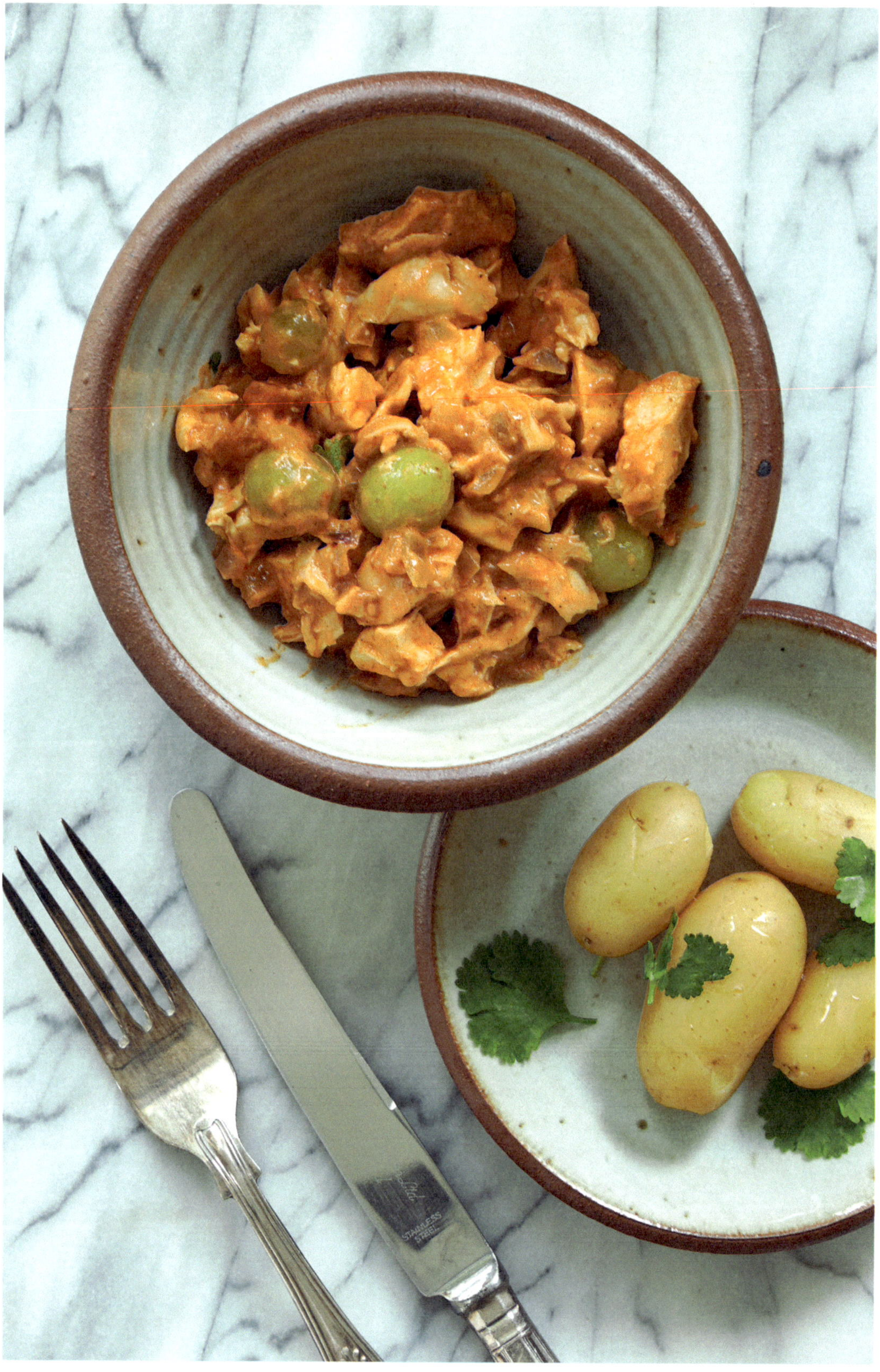
STAINLESS STEEL

DINNER
12

Celebration Chicken

Every Brit knows what a Coronation Chicken is. For the first time, pieces of cold roast chicken in curry mayonnaise sauce were served at a banquet in honour of the coronation of Elizabeth II in 1953.

SERVES 4

1 medium chicken

TO MAKE THE SAUCE

No more than 230 ml of water
½ jar (220 g) of mango chutney
Any large pieces of mango should be chopped
2 tbsp olive oil
1 medium onion, chopped
6 heaped tsp tomato puree
4 heaped tbsp mayonnaise
3 heaped tsp Madras curry powder
A dash of lemon juice

1. Begin by roasting a chicken. When cooked, remove the meat from the bones and chop into bite-sized chunks.
2. Sweat the onion in olive oil until translucent. Remove from the heat and add the curry powder, tomato puree, lemon juice and water. Bring to the boil and then reduce the heat. Cover the pan and simmer for 15 minutes. Remove and allow to cool in a glass bowl.
3. When cooled, mix sufficient curry mix into the mayonnaise to make a pink, tasty sauce, then add the mango chutney. Finally add the chicken to the sauce.
4. Serve with new potatoes and a colourful salad.

Heather likes to add a few green seedless grapes to the chicken.

This recipe was given to Heather by a chef. It is so much nicer than the standard coronation chicken and makes a lovely summer meal to share with friends or as a very smart picnic dish.

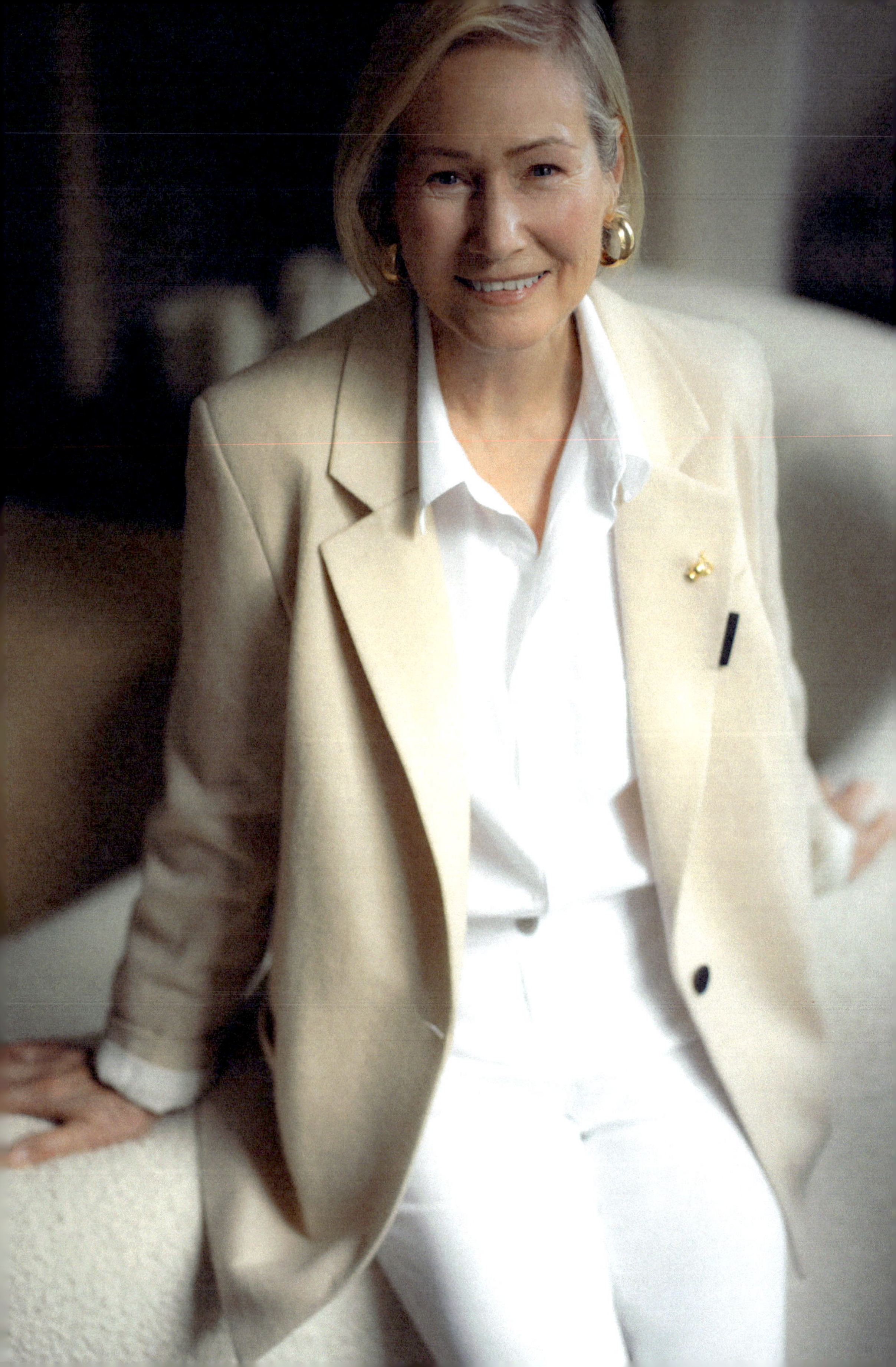

Heather talks

INDEPENDENCE AND HAPPINESS

Now, I prefer relationships without any obligations. I've given away half of everything twice because I've been married twice. I've ended it both times. Having to start over and have less than you put in – I am not going to do that again. I've worked my way back up to a nice house, nice garden, no money worries, no debts, and I don't want to put all that at risk. What I have now, I want to leave to my son.

I don't need a man to provide for me, to look after me. I look after myself. I drive a car, I can change a tyre, fix something in the house, paint rooms, light a fire. I value independence. So, if a man is in my life, it's on my terms.

For me, it is not necessary to feel myself in love with someone. I have male friends, I can always ring up somebody and say, 'Fancy going out?' or, 'Shall we go for a walk?'

I think nobody else is responsible for your happiness, only you are responsible for that. You can get pleasure, excitement, and fun from all sorts of different places. You don't need a man to do that for you.

One day, I was very surprised when, before a date, I saw Heather in ordinary clothes (in which she could work in the garden), barefoot and without jewellery. I asked when she would change her clothes. Heather replied that she couldn't cook and dress up at the same time. If the man does not take her to a restaurant today, he will not see her in all her glory.

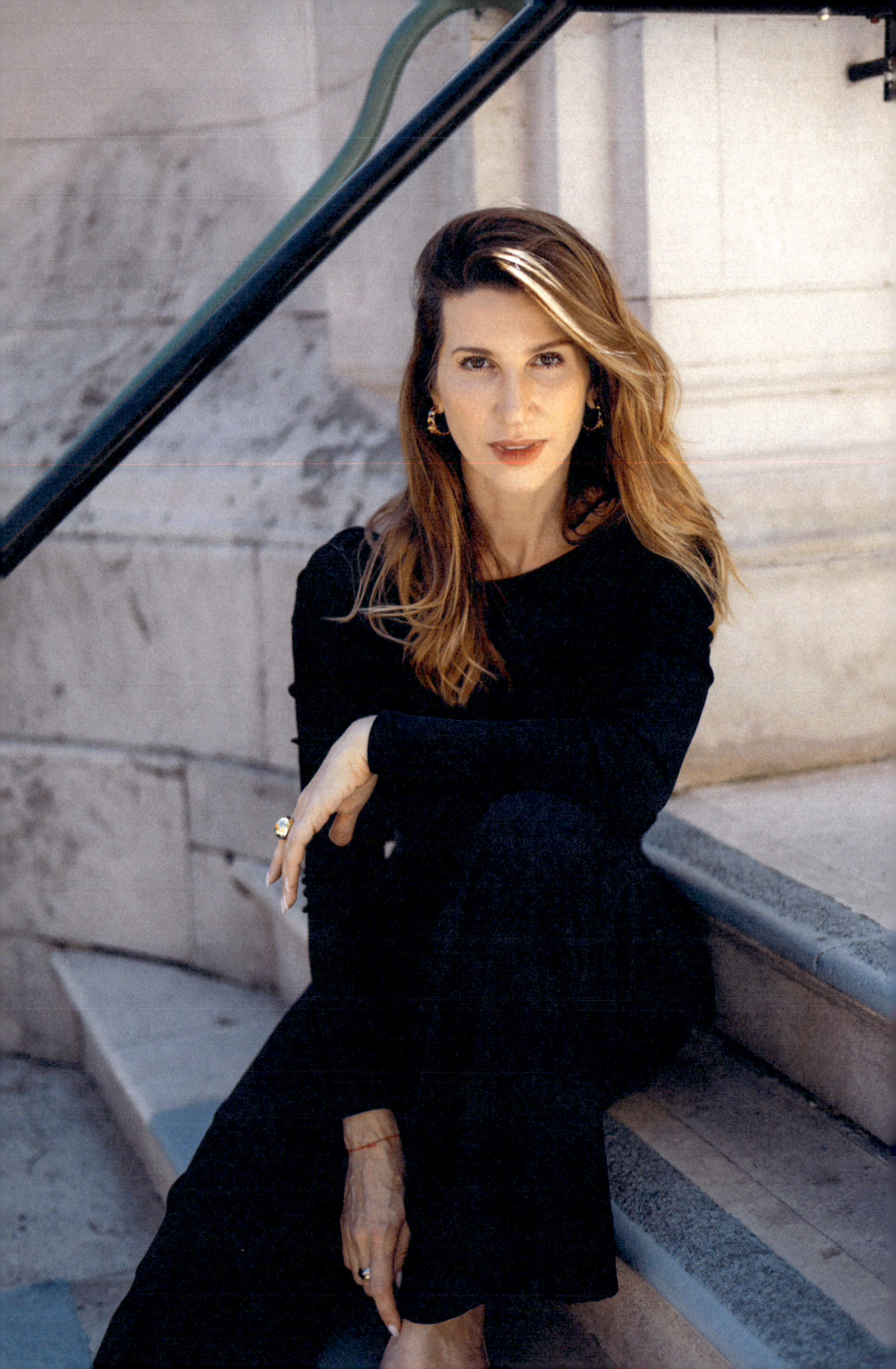

Did you know that...

The British are used to saving money on heating.
Cold? Put on another sweater. Blue lips at night? Take another blanket and a heating pad. The most popular heating pads here are old-fashioned rubber ones, filled with hot water, in covers made of artificial fur. They are called hot water bottles. Heroically freezing and not pretending to be cold seems to be a national sport.
In winter, people are outside in sneakers, ballet flats, and even shorts. Hats and umbrellas are often ignored.

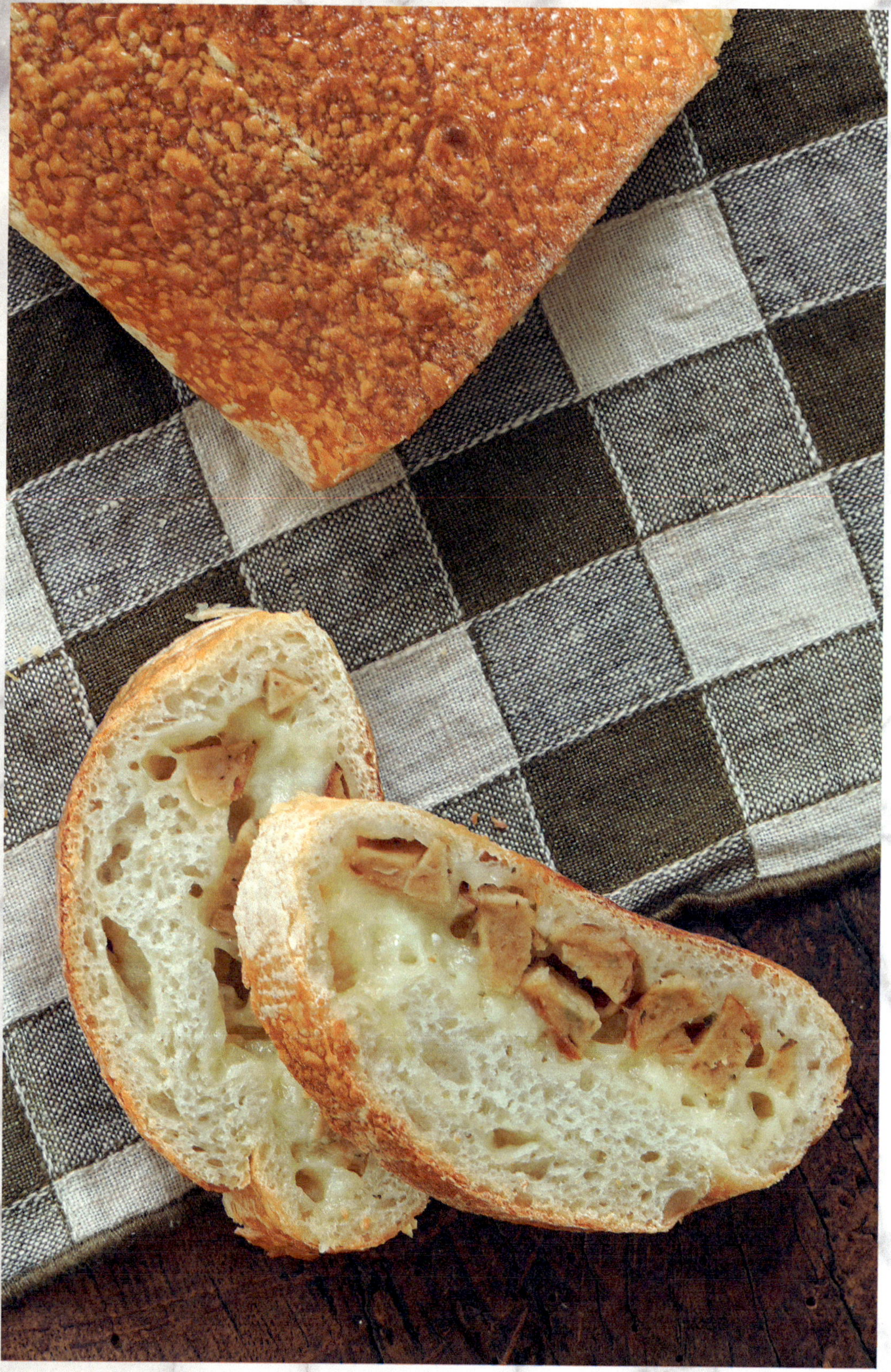

DINNER 13

Italian Sausage Bread

Sausage rolls are one of the most popular snacks in Great Britain. This recipe was shared with Heather by her old friend from America when her son Daniel was young. It is still a firm favourite with him, and now with her grandchildren as well.

SERVES 4

600-700 g sausages
500 g pizza or bread dough
100-120 g mozzarella cheese
30 g parmesan
1 egg, beaten
Pizza sauce for dipping

1. Begin by cooking the sausages, then remove the skins and roughly chop the meat.
2. Roll out the dough on a floured surface until it is about 10 cm wide and 30-35 cm long.
3. Brush with the egg, reserving some for the outside of the roll. Spread the sausage meat and grated cheese down the centre of the dough. Fold the ends up over the filling and then one side over the other, sealing with the egg. Brush the top of the loaf with egg and cook at 180°C for 30 minutes until golden brown.
4. Serve hot in chunky slices with pizza sauce for dipping.

Vegetarian sausages work just as well in this recipe.

For this recipe, Heather likes to use thick pork sausages with herbs or chilli in them, but it's your choice, whichever you prefer.

Daniel

Heather talks

CHILDREN AND FOOD

Children can often be difficult with their food. I don't think you need to put a lot of stress and pressure on either you or your child. Mealtime should be fun. It should just be time for laughing around the table. I think children pick up on mothers who are stressed about, 'they've got to eat this, they've got to eat that', and the children then don't want to. It's fine, they won't starve, they'll come when they're hungry.

My friend had a child who refused to eat for a long time when he was quite little. She used to hide food around the house and then watched him. And he began sneaking around eating it. So, she knew he was eating.

I always had a problem with my son eating fruits – Daniel wasn't very good at that. I remember I did 'meet a new fruit' week, when each day of the week I would bring him some sort of exotic fruit that he had never tried before. In the end, my son said, 'Please don't do it anymore, my friends won't come here'. Other than that, I think I did my best for him.

I didn't give my son a vegetarian diet, so he got all the nutrition he needed: vegetables and the fruits but also meat. He was quite slim and fit – very active and sporty. In his thirties he started to put on a lot of weight. And he noticed that I didn't. 'That might be something in your diet, mum. I think I'll try it', he said. So, he became vegetarian too. But then had to change his diet after his gall bladder operation and now he eats fish, and occasionally chicken, like me.

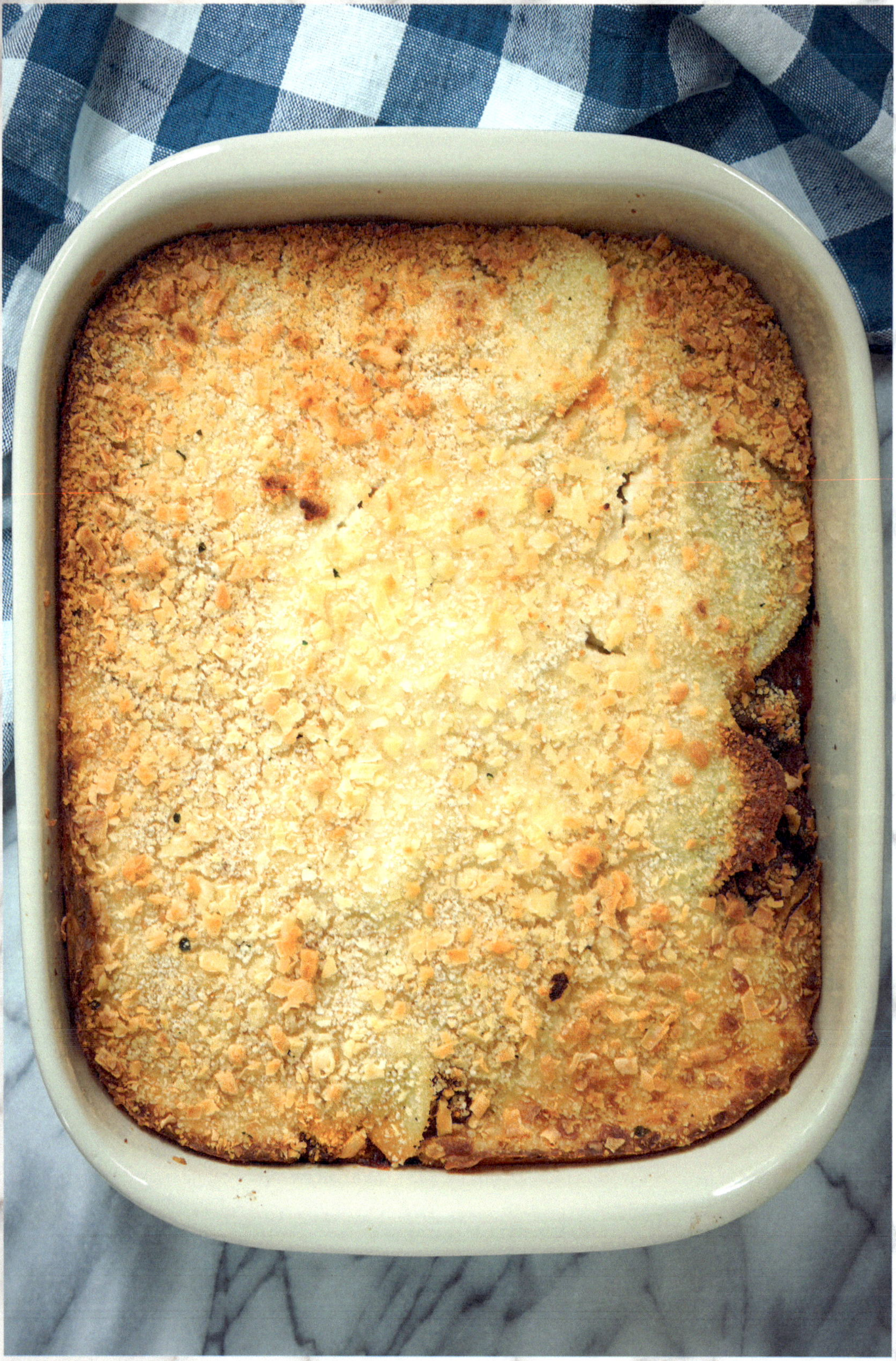

DINNER
14

Vegetarian Moussaka

There are as many versions of moussaka as there are stars in the sky, and this is Heather's own amalgamation of various vegetarian recipes that she has tried over the years.

SERVES 4

500 g cooked potatoes, medium sliced
500 g Quorn mince
400 g can of chopped tomatoes
200 ml red wine
3-4 medium aubergines, medium sliced
2 medium onions, chopped
2 cloves of garlic, crushed
Olive oil
2 dessert spoons of tomato puree
2 tsp dried oregano
2 tsp ground cinnamon
2 bay leaves
Pepper

TOPPING

500 g natural creamy Greek yoghurt
3 medium eggs
2 dessert spoons of flour
A pinch of baking powder
Grated nutmeg to taste

1. Fry the slices of aubergine in oil in batches for 5-7 minutes until golden brown, then allow to drain on kitchen paper.
2. Next, sauté the onions until soft and transparent; add the garlic, tomato puree tomatoes, herbs, red wine and Quorn mince.
3. Simmer uncovered until the sauce has thickened, stirring occasionally.
4. Then, in a greased baking dish, assemble the moussaka in layers like a lasagna. Begin with a layer of the Quorn mixture, followed by a layer of potatoes, then a layer of aubergines, and another layer of Quorn. Finally, add whatever is left of the potatoes and aubergines.
5. Finish by mixing the topping ingredients together and pouring over the top of the dish. Bake at 200°C (180°C fan) in the centre of the oven for about 35-40 minutes until a deep golden brown. If it browns too much, cover with foil.

If you are feeling lazy and want to skip a step, use tinned potatoes and slice them. Also, if Quorn is not for you, you can use brown lentils instead.

And to save time, rather than frying the aubergines, slice them, put them in a baking tray, drizzle with olive oil, and bake in the oven.

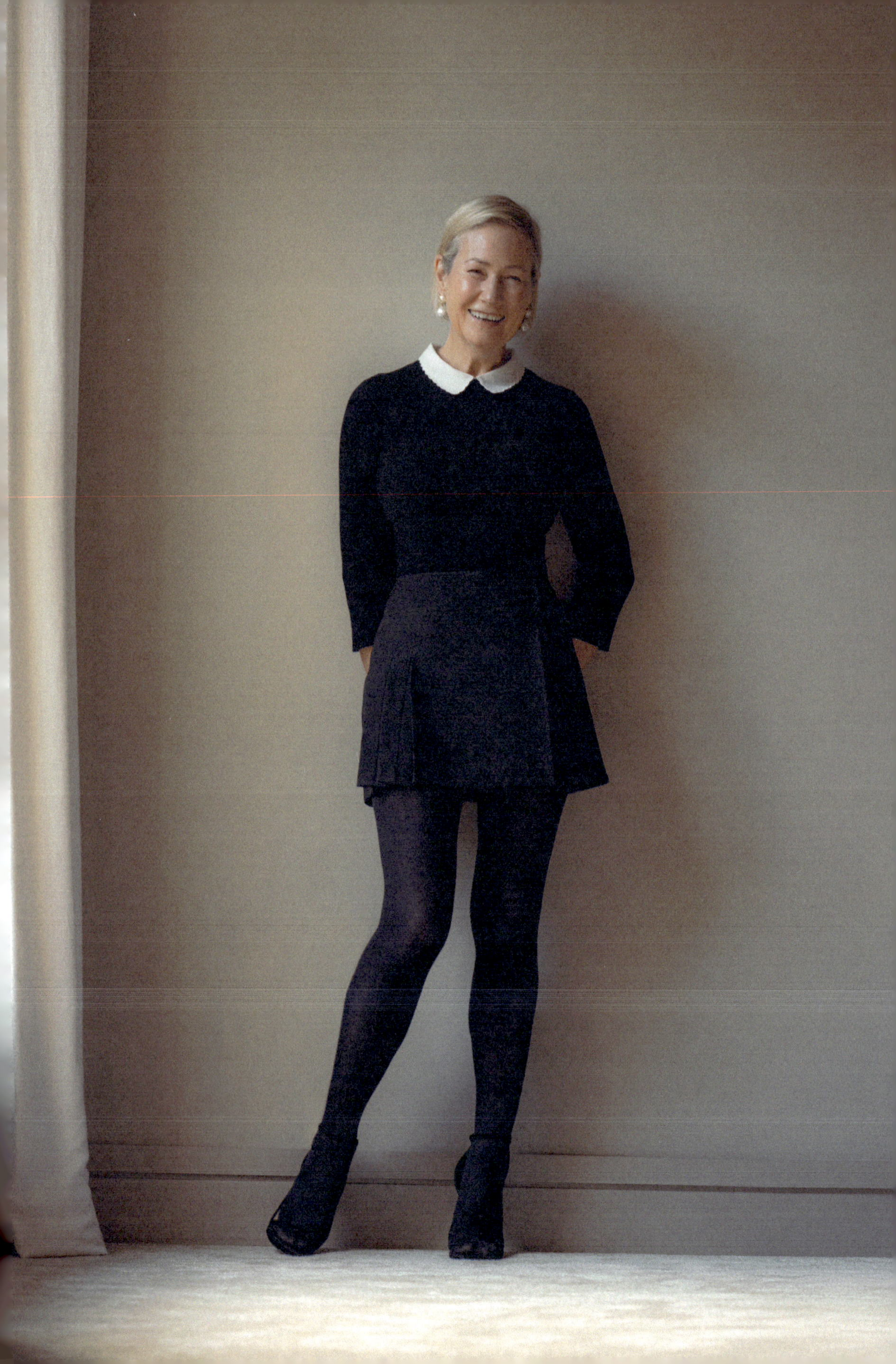

Heather talks

DANCING AND FRIENDSHIP

When I was young, I was at ballet school for a long time. And I continued to take ballet classes even when I was an adult – just to stay fit. Then I did salsa for a little while. Dancing is something I enjoy as a form of exercise. I think if you dance when you're young, it leaves its mark on your body: you are still flexible when you are older; it sort of stretches you out.

Now, I walk a lot. I walk for 2 hours or so every day if the weather is nice. I don't wear a fitness tracker; I just know how many steps it is by the amount of time it takes. I can do 10,000 easily. When I went to Italy last year with my friend, we walked so much. One day, it was something like 17,000 steps. Of course, that was in high heels! Do you doubt it?

Where else do I take my energy from? I don't know; I still feel 17 inside. I just don't feel any different to the way I did when I was young. I get bored easily and I can't sit still. I always need to be doing something. I like to laugh. The friends who make me laugh make me feel like that. I joke that I have an active social life: six days out of seven are always planned.

I have lots of friends, and we go back years. Some of them I have known for 73 years! We lived around the corner from each other, two sisters and me. Then we went to primary school together. There are friends from grammar school, friends from uni, friends from work... I just collect them and keep them. Friends are the family you choose. They are really important to me.

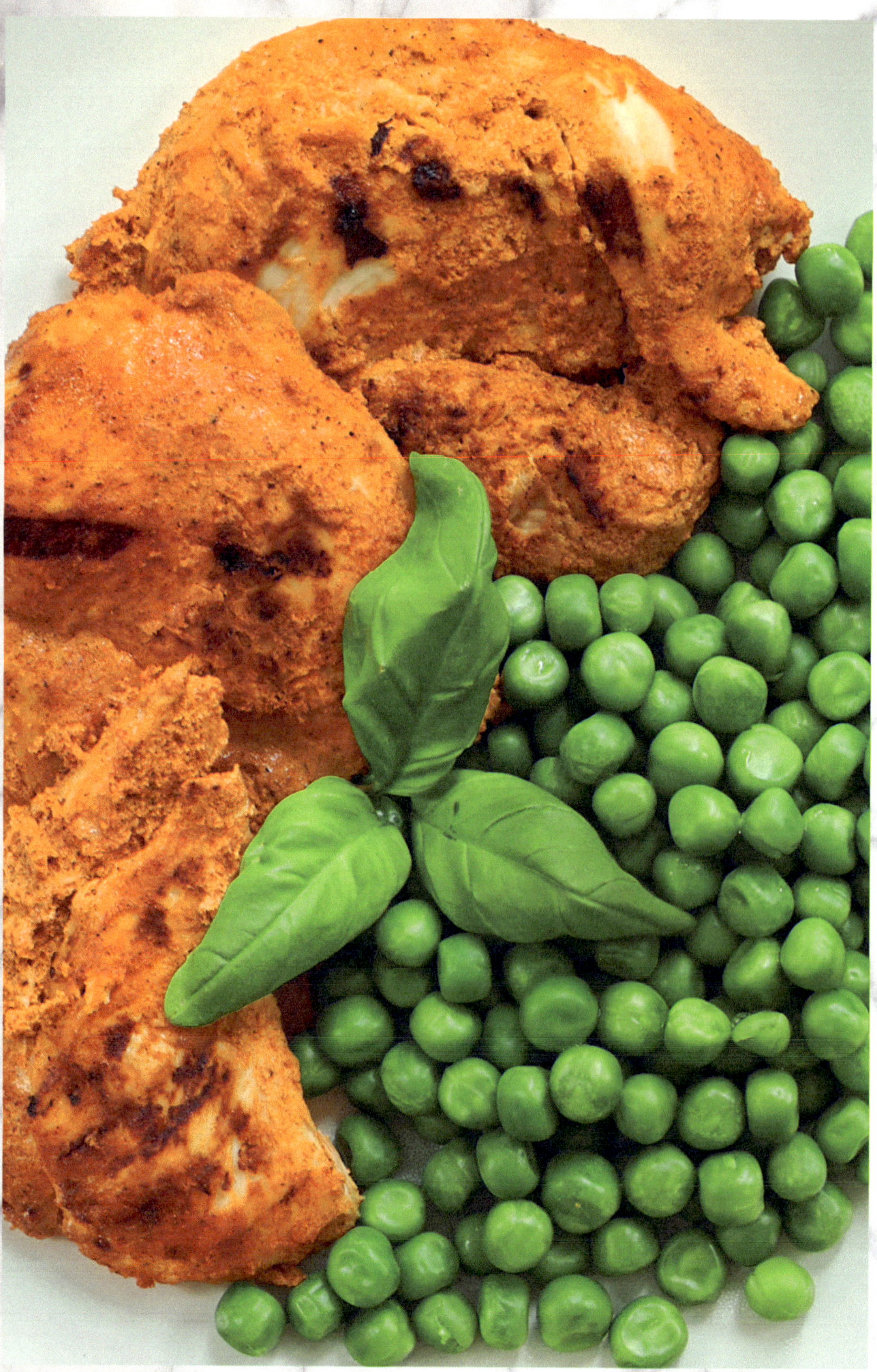

DINNER
15

Tandoori Chicken

This BBQ recipe was shared with Heather by her neighbour and friend, who is an excellent cook herself. It is simple and quick to make the marinade for chicken which makes the meat both succulent and super tasty. It never fails to impress – lifting a BBQ above the usual burgers and sausages.

SERVES 4

4 chicken breasts (500 g)

FOR MARINADE:
500 g natural yoghurt
Juice of 1½-2 lemons
4 large tbsp tandoori spice mix
2 large tbsp vegetable oil

1. Mix the marinade ingredients together.
2. Butterfly the chicken breasts *(i.e., cut almost through lengthwise and open up)*.
3. Add the chicken to the marinade and coat well. Marinade in zip-lock bags in the fridge for 24 hours *(or at this point, it can be frozen until needed)*.
4. Cook on a BBQ for about 5 minutes on each side, or until chicken is cooked through.
5. Serve with new potatoes and salad.

Depending on the season, roast in the oven or grill – tandoori will be the star of any barbecue party and a great way to add variety to the usual menu of burgers and sausages.

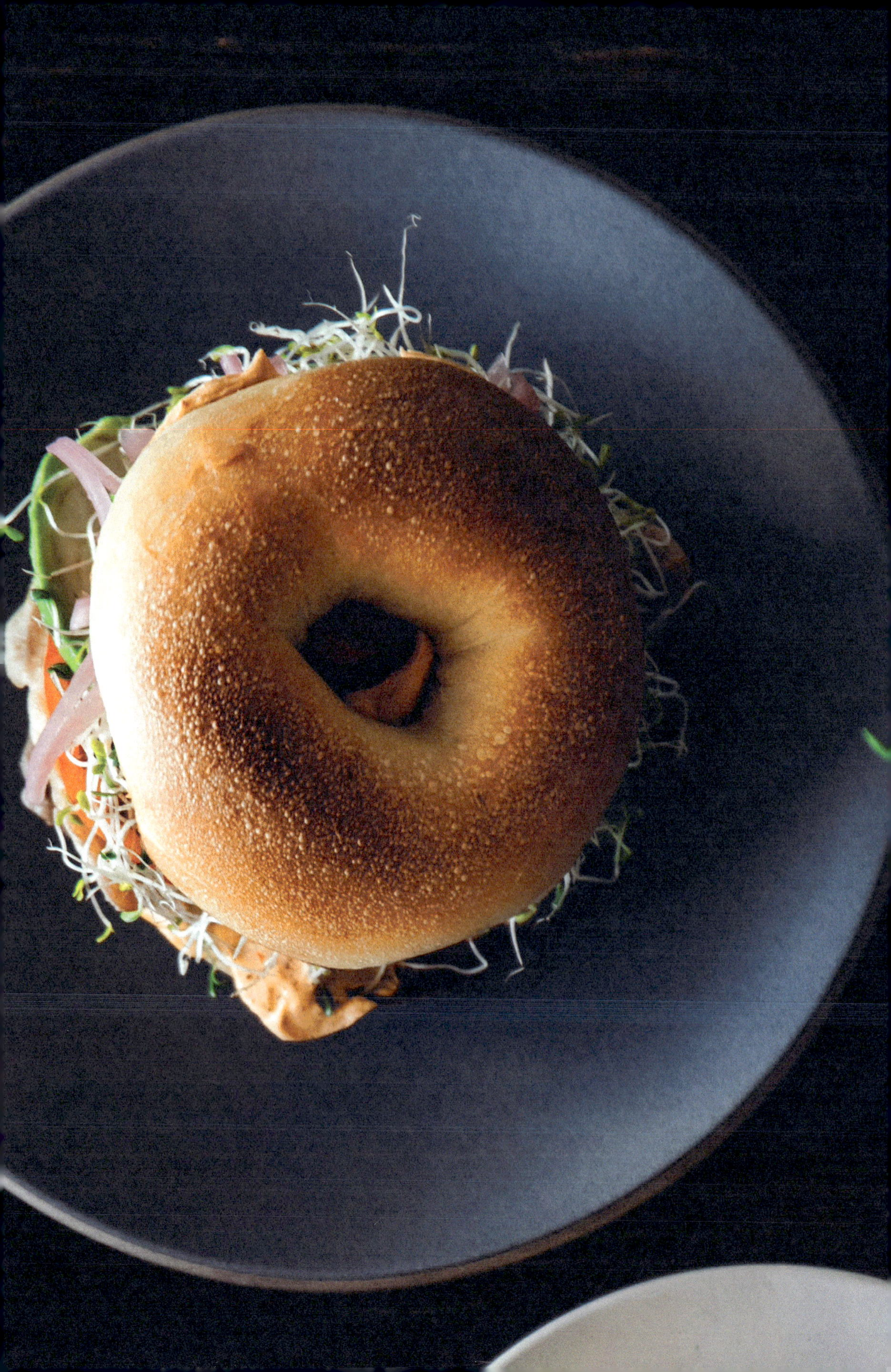

Heather talks

WEIGHT AND CARBOHYDRATES

I've managed to stay the same weight of 58.5 kg, size S, since I was about 16. Perhaps my eating habits, not eating after 7 p.m. and skipping breakfast, help with this. As I have said, I only eat carbs at lunchtime – never in the evening. I prefer bread with lots of wholegrains, and seeds and nuts. I can fill my lunch sandwiches with eggs, cheese, prawns, green salad, coleslaw, vegetables, Quorn veggie meat, dill pickles, chutney, hot chillies and jalapeños.

MY 5 FAVOURITE LUNCHES ARE:

1. A Greek meze of tzatziki, houmous, olives, carrot batons, and pita bread.
2. Toasted bagels with cream cheese, smoked salmon, and a squeeze of lemon juice.
3. A toasted cheese sandwich.
4. Spicy parsnip soup and crusty bread.
5. An old-fashioned ploughman's lunch: crusty bread, strong cheese, pickles, and apple slices + tea with milk.

DESSERTS

Heather doesn't have a sweet tooth. She could leave sweets and chocolate in the cupboard for weeks and they wouldn't tempt her. She makes great desserts, but rarely eats them herself. At a restaurant, she can order a starter and a main course, but she will most likely skip dessert, or have cheese. She likes to make desserts like lemon cheesecake, which can be frozen and defrosted when needed – it saves time and effort. This recipe, and a few more of Heather's beautiful desserts, can be found on the following pages.

A very Scottish dessert! Traditionally served as an end to the Burns Night meal or at any other time of the year, especially when raspberries are in season and at their cheapest. It is better not to make this dessert too far in advance of serving.

Cranachan

SERVES 4

375 ml double cream
300 g raspberries
3 tbsp rolled oats
2 tbsp honey
2 tbsp whiskey
1 tsp caster sugar

1. Take care to save some oats and whole raspberries for topping.
2. Toast the oats by lining a baking tray with baking parchment. Sprinkle the oats in an even layer and roast for approximately 5 minutes in a moderate oven until they are crunchy, golden, and smell nice and nutty. Leave to cool.
3. Push half the raspberries through a sieve into a bowl. Sweeten to taste with sugar.
4. Whisk the cream until it forms soft peaks and fold in the whiskey and honey.
5. Assemble the oats, raspberry sauce, and cream in layers in decorative glasses.

Heather talks

COLOURFUL FOOD AND THE UK'S CUISINE

I think you eat with the eye as much as with the mouth. You have to want to eat when you look at the plate. So, if you have a plain plate, put colourful food on it. Make it look nice.

I have always liked vegetables and they are naturally colourful. I don't like beige food, or bland, one-colour dishes. Salads and fresh raw veg look lovely. I like the displays in supermarkets with all the fresh veg. I will eat any kind of salad you put in front of me. In fact, when I go to restaurants, I choose salads – exotic salads that I probably wouldn't make for myself. Just because I like vegetables, the look of them, the taste of them.

If we speak about traditional English cuisine, I can't really think of anything apart from the Sunday roast dinner and fish & chips. But in fact, it's so much more than that. Our food has come a long way. It has formed from a mixture of other cultures because we have so many different nationalities in the UK.

So, our cuisine has taken things from different countries and absorbed them. I grew up in London, and even way back when I was a child, we had Chinese restaurants there. And, of course, we love Indian food; there is an Indian restaurant on every corner.

This dessert has long been associated with Eton College due to it always being served at the annual cricket match at Lord's between Eton and Harrow. Comprising basically of just 3 main ingredients, it is a very traditional dessert which is universally loved by adults and children alike. Your children will also love making this as it is quick, easy, and there is no cooking involved.

Eton Mess

SERVES 4-6

500 g strawberries
5 ready-made meringue nests
580 ml double cream
2 tbsp icing sugar

1. Blend about ⅓ of the strawberries with ½ the icing sugar to make a strawberry sauce.
2. Roughly chop the rest of the strawberries. Whip the cream with the other ½ of the icing sugar until it forms soft peaks. Roughly crush 4 of the meringue nests. Then fold the strawberries, cream, and meringue together.
3. Finally, swirl the strawberry sauce through and serve in pretty glasses or bowls with the remaining meringue crushed and sprinkled over the top.

One word of warning, however – do not make it too far in advance. It is best eaten as soon after making as possible, so that the meringue remains crunchy.

Heather talks

WINE AND THE TRADITION OF AFTERNOON TEA

I have one of my cups of filtered coffee in the morning, and then I have tea at lunchtime. No milk in coffee and always milk in tea. The only tea I drink without milk is Earl Grey because it's not meant to be drunk with milk; it's very fragrant, scented.

Mostly in the evening I have a glass of wine-or two. I like Prosecco or Aperol Spritz when it's nice and sunny in the garden. Spirits? No, I just don't like the taste. I have gin & tonic occasionally with my son and daughter-in-law. But they pour gin into a tumbler and I only have that little screw cap on a gin bottle, and the rest is tonic.

You told me you heard about the English tradition of 5 o'clock tea. It's one of those that has died out because people lived differently when they used to have tea at 4.30. In the past, they would have a big breakfast, then they would have lunch, and then dinner wouldn't be until very late – at 8 p.m. But people don't eat like that anymore. I think they eat less now than they used to. And people's lives are just too busy to stop for tea. So, it's very difficult to fit in today.

But it's a nice tradition occasionally when you try it. You can have tea in some beautiful place like the Ritz in London. They serve it with scones and tiny little sandwiches and little cakes. In Devon and Cornwall, they have cream tea with scones, clotted cream, and jam. I love that. There are a lot of debates about whether to spread the scone with jam or cream first, but from a practical point of view, you can't really spread jam on top of cream. So, if you spread the jam on the scone and then spoon the cream on top that works better, that's all.

This recipe was given to Heather by a friend who said that one slice of this cake daily helped to relieve menopausal symptoms. We can only assume that this is due to the soya which is supposed to be helpful. However, I like the idea of a cake that is good for you.

HRT* Cake

SERVES 8

230 g raisins
Approx 150 ml soya milk
115 g soya flour
115 g whole wheat flour
115 g porridge oats
115 g linseeds
55 g sunflower seeds
55 g pumpkin seeds
55 g sesame seeds
55 g flaked almonds
2 pieces of stem ginger, chopped
1 tbsp malt extract
½ tsp ground ginger
½ tsp cinnamon
½ tsp nutmeg

1. Put the dry ingredients into a large bowl and mix thoroughly. Add soya milk and malt extract. Mix well and leave to soak for half an hour. If the mixture is too stiff, add more soya milk.
2. Spoon into a loaf tin lined with oiled baking parchment. Bake at 190°C for about 75 minutes. Turn out and leave to cool.
3. Serve in slices with butter and jam.

HRT – Hormone Replacement Therapy

Heather talks

THE PEOPLE OF GREAT BRITAIN

I think people here are quite polite, they wouldn't be rude or abrupt. We are not very good with other languages; we tend to think everybody speaks English, which is a bit arrogant.

I'm often very grateful to live in England. We're very lucky in many ways. We don't have extreme weather, nasty snakes or insects. We have a peaceful country and in this world that's a huge blessing. We have long memories; our parents' generation remembers the war. We have a great sympathy for people from Ukraine who are suffering now.

I think we are empathetic and kind people. We like to drink. We like to party. But generally, we aren't bad people.

They say that British teenagers are breaking away like no other. I think they get to the point where they can see their independence on the horizon and they want to push all of the boundaries, all of the rules in that struggle to be an independent adult. My own son went through that. He used to go out and drink, get drunk; it was a nightmare. He did go quite wild for a little while. But all of my friends said, 'Don't worry, he will come back – all the things you taught him will finally sink in'. And by the age of 21, he was a nice responsible guy.

I remember one of my elderly friends said to me one day, 'Oh, I saw Daniel at church the other day. He's so charming, so polite'. And I thought, 'No, you've got the wrong child'. I think they save all that aggression and wildness for their parents because they know we are always there and forgive them.

Lemon Cheesecake

This no-bake cheesecake is light, fresh tasting and freezes really well. It originally came from a friend at work nearly 50 years ago and has been made by Heather over the years more times than she can count. It never fails to please.

SERVES 8

230 g cottage cheese
170 g crushed digestive biscuits
120 g fresh cream cheese
120 g caster sugar
60-80 g butter
2 eggs, separated
140 ml double cream lightly beaten
15 g powdered gelatine
Rind and juice of a lemon
Salt to taste

1. Melt the butter over a low heat. Remove from the heat and stir in the crushed digestive biscuits and 30 g of the sugar. Then press the mixture over the base of an 20 cm loose-bottomed cake tin and put in the fridge to set.
2. Put 3 tbsp of cold water in a pan and sprinkle gelatine evenly over the surface. Set aside to soak for a few minutes.
3. Rub the cottage cheese through a coarse sieve and mix thoroughly with the cream cheese and finely grated lemon rind.
4. Put the egg yolks in a separate bowl, add 40 g of caster sugar and a pinch of salt. Beat until light and creamy.
5. Gently heat the gelatine, stirring continuously. Do not allow it to boil. When dissolved, remove from the heat and add the strained lemon juice.
6. Whisk this liquid into the egg yolks and then blend into the cheese mixture.
7. Whisk the egg whites until stiff and fold in the remaining sugar. Fold the lightly beaten cream and then the egg whites into the cheese mixture and pour onto the chilled biscuit base. Refrigerate for 2-3 hours until set. Remove from the tin and decorate. Heather often uses blueberries, strawberries, or tinned mandarins.
8. This freezes well too.

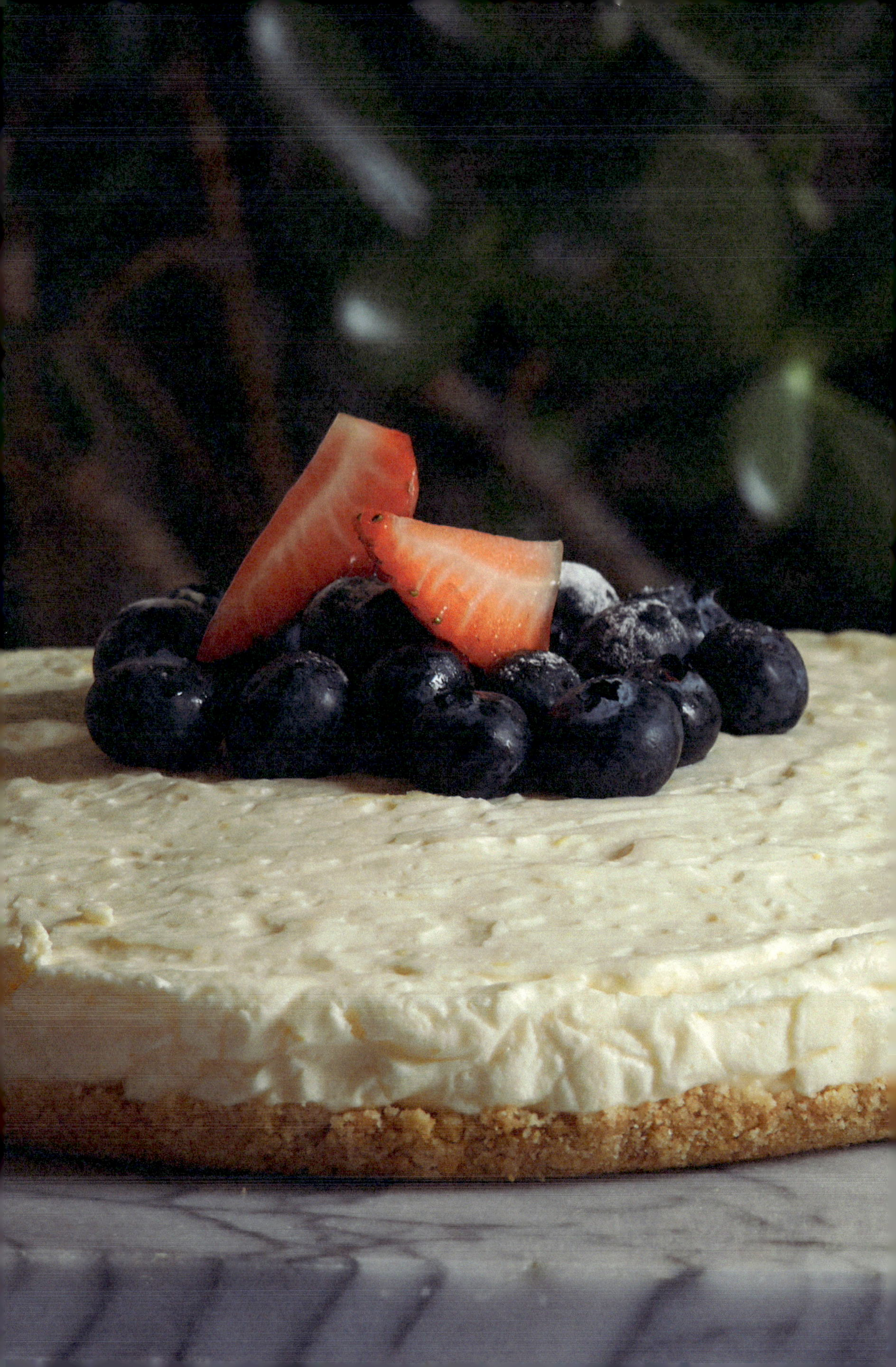

" IF EVERY PERSON COULD *make it a better place* BY SMALL THINGS, IT *would be a much nicer world*, WOULDN'T IT?

Heather talks

MAKING THE WORLD A BETTER PLACE

Living with my grandparents, I was not allowed to eat until the animals were fed. My grandmother said, 'They can't do that themselves; they depend on us. We must do that for them first'.

We also have this memory of the war. My family was in London so they were constantly being bombed. My mother was a Marine Wren, my father was in the Royal Navy, and my grandparents were volunteers. So that memory was passed down to me when I came along just after the war. Perhaps because we remember, we are empathetic to other people who are going through these things now, which they never should be.

I think we learn to give from our early days. Back then we were always encouraged at the church to give – to people who survived disasters, to children who didn't have schooling in other countries. It is embedded in our culture; you help others if you can. People of a certain age volunteer when they retire and have more time, but still want to do something. I used to volunteer at a school in America when I was underemployed. My stepson and my son were at school, my husband was at work, and it was just me and my dog. I didn't have enough to do, so I volunteered.

It is simple: if you can donate to charity, give your time or welcome people into your home, then do it. We're not on this earth for very long and if every person can make it a better place by doing the small things, it would be a much nicer world, you know?

Summer Pudding

This is the quintessential English dessert, originating in the 19th century as diet food, as the bread was less fattening than pastry. It still brings back memories of Heather's grandmother making this for her when summer fruits were plentiful from allotments or gardens in the seemingly endless summer holidays.

SERVES 4-6

750 g mixed summer fruits *(i.e., raspberries, blackberries, blueberries, redcurrants, blackcurrants, stoned cherries)*
An additional 150 g of raspberries and 150 g of strawberries, hulled and sliced *(do not cook these)*
Approx 8 slices of white bread *(crusts removed)*
125 g golden caster sugar
½ an orange *(zest and juice)*

1. Begin by lining a 1-litre pudding basin with a double layer of cling film, which should overlap well over the sides of the basin.
2. Next, gently cook the mixed berries, sugar, orange juice, and zest until the berries release their juice, taking care to stir gently so the berries remain whole if possible.
3. When cool, stir in the additional raspberries and strawberries, strain the fruit through a sieve, and reserve. Put the juice in a shallow dish.
4. Quickly dip one side of each piece of bread in the juice and line the base and sides of the basin with the bread, dipped side facing outwards. Cut to fit, but do not leave any gaps.
5. Fill with the reserved fruits and trim the edges of the bread to the top of the basin. Put a lid of bread on top of the fruit and pour over any remaining juice. Then place a saucer that fits just inside the bowl on top of the upper layer of bread and weigh it down with something heavy *(for example, a tin of beans or bag of rice)*.
6. Cool in the fridge overnight.
7. The next day, remove the weight and saucer and put a serving plate over the top of the basin.
8. Invert the pudding, ease off the basin and remove the cling film. Serve cut in thick slices with double cream and extra fruit if desired.

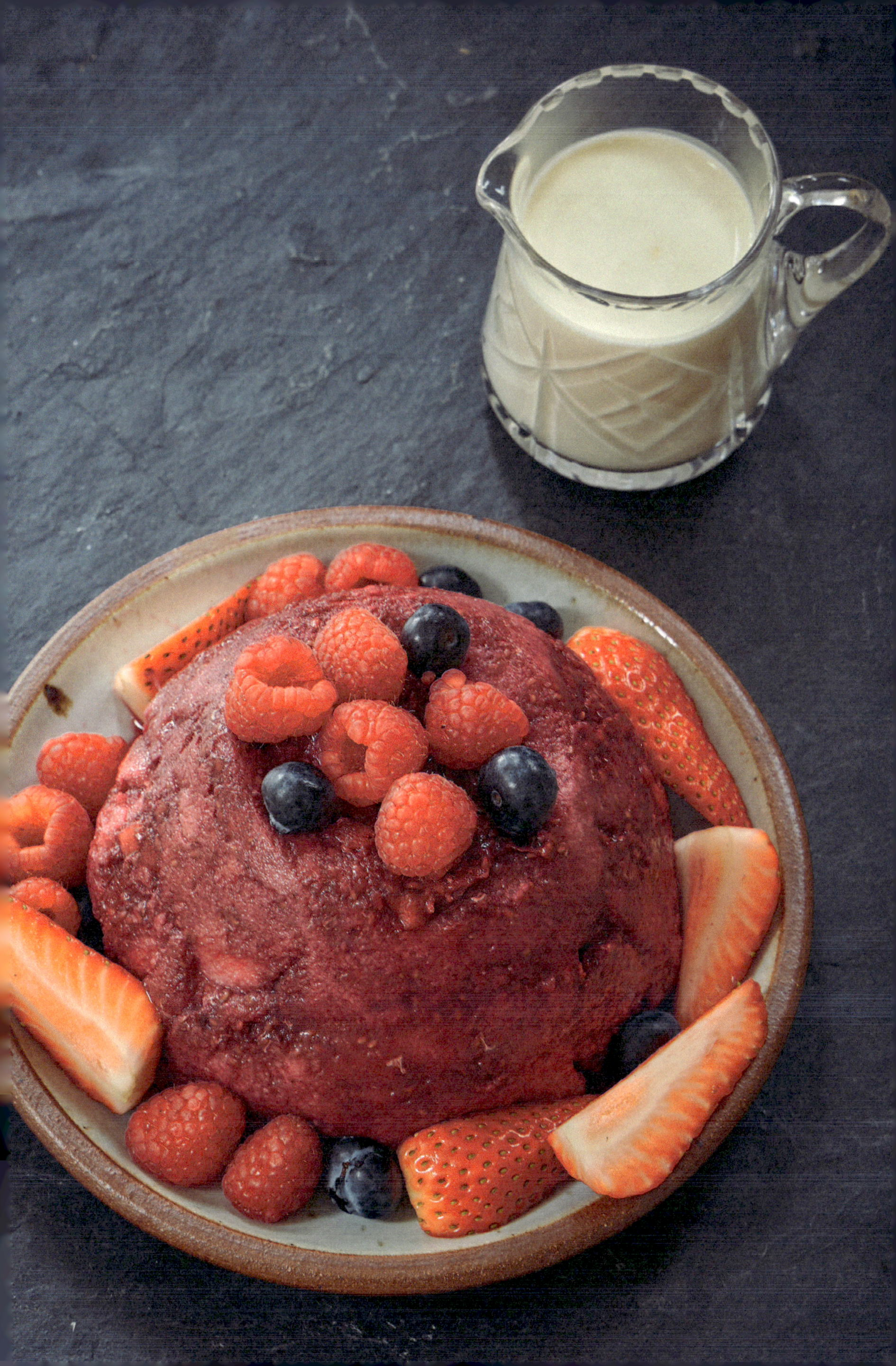

HEATHER — A WOMAN OF TREASURE

The profound insight that came to me with Heather entering my life was that when I think about old age, I feel a sense of dread. This is not the fear of wrinkles on my face, nor the fear of becoming uninteresting or ceasing to learn, although that is certainly part of it. It is the fear of finding myself in the midst of my life without the energy to live it fully.

There is no trace in Heather of any 'whiff of exhaustion with life', be that in her house, her bedroom, or in herself. This was perhaps what inspired me to write this book. I realised that at any age that it is our habits that shape us and how we feel.

HEATHER'S HABITS:

Total cleanliness in everything: from the fridge and the garden shed to the tips of her nails and her thoughts.

1. Perfectly clean clothes, immediately ironed after washing, including socks.
2. Hair washed every other day.
3. Thoroughly brushing her teeth and rinsing twice a day.
4. Well-ventilated rooms and a made bed *(with a change of linen every 10 days)*.

DIETARY HABITS AND PHYSICAL ACTIVITY:

1. A two-hour walk in nature at least twice a week.
2. No excess weight of 1-2 pounds allowed. Heather's weight is 130 pounds and she is 5 feet 6 inches tall.
3. Dietary restrictions before holidays so she can eat more than usual with the family during celebrations.
4. No red meat and never eating after 7 p.m.

BODY CARE:

1. Body scrub twice a week with a loofah.
2. Facial scrub once a week.
3. Never leave the shower without deeply moisturising with body cream.
4. Hair highlighted every six weeks *(booked in advance)*.
5. Perfume: Chanel No. 5.
6. Cuticle oil, lip moisturiser, and hand cream before bed. All these are on her bedside table.

LOVE AND SOCIAL ACTIVITY:

1. Travel plans made a year in advance.
2. Scheduled social activities – interactions and experiences planned a month ahead.
3. Interaction with people who make her laugh.
4. She loves men younger than herself in vintage cars, in the 'silver fox' style *(tall, grey-haired, a 'bad boy')*.
5. Economical in everyday purchases and very generous in all matters concerning emotions and other people.
6. Regular sex.

ATMOSPHERE AND MOOD:

1. No tired groans when sitting or lying down.
2. Constant sharp yet kind humour with close ones.
3. A smile with a hint of flirtation in her eyes and movements.
4. Daily reading of literary fiction and cognitive development with the New York Times app – Wordle *(to solve the word of the day)*.
5. White silk pyjamas at night *(camisole and shorts)*.

When I asked Heather what she thought of 'granny pants', she replied that she doesn't think about them because her underwear is just like mine, provided mine aren't 'granny style', but lacy and sexy.

Anita Lutsenko

YOU'RE NEVER TOO OLD FOR ANYTHING

Editor: Natalia Pasichnyk
Design: Antonina Latayko
Photo: Katerina Astrella, Mariana Shafro, Barney Hindle
Proofreading: Barney Ellis